Through the Eyes of a Child

Through the Eyes of a Child

Encounters with God in the Middle East

ISBN: 979-8-9884517-0-9

Library of Congress Control Number: 2023909786

Open your mouth for the people who cannot speak,
For the rights of all the unfortunate.
Open your mouth, judge righteously,
And defend the rights of the poor and needy.

Proverbs 31:8-9 (NASB)

CONTENTS

INTRODUCTION

Childhood is a fleeting, formative time. A time of transition from complete dependence on others to hopeful independence and self-sufficiency. A time of potential and promise. A time of wonder and growth when seeds of identity take root.

A time of vulnerability.

Across the globe, all children navigate the joys, struggles, and pitfalls of their journey toward adulthood; they navigate circumstances that deeply influence them. Where they grow up, the cultural moment in which they live, the resources available to them, and the choices of those around them all have an impact on a child's development—physical, mental, emotional, relational, and even spiritual.

But the experiences of children growing up in the war-torn Middle East and North Africa (MENA) differ from those of other children across the world. Unlike in the West, where much of the cultural messaging centers around the individual, in the MENA region, social formation revolves around the community. Society places expectations on children at an early age so that they act in ways that best represent those around them. Should children go against these societal expectations to pursue their own desires, they could bring shame upon themselves, their family, and their community—a product of living within an honor-shame culture.

In an honor-shame culture, society weighs an individual's every action. This watchfulness breeds fear, secrecy, and pride, evils hostile to holy living. As one MENA believer shared, "The great persecution of the Church in this region is not that the believer might be killed for their faith, but that

1

their faith might be stifled by the honor-shame system."

Not only do MENA children grapple with the everyday struggles of childhood within the bounds of an honor-shame code of conduct, but many contend with the traumas of war, hunger, and displacement, too. Oftentimes, their voices go unheard, their stories untold. But with this book, Ananias House seeks to change that.

The following ten stories, inspired by real people Ananias House has encountered throughout its ministry in the MENA region, provide insight into the lives and thoughts of children who may otherwise go unheard. While these stories may prove difficult to journey through at times—*this book contains scenes and insinuations of violence which may be offensive to some readers and is inappropriate for children*—they offer a glimpse into the daily realities of young people in one of the most dangerous parts of the world. Some stories highlight the impact of war, displacement, natural disaster, economic collapse, relational sin, and extreme poverty, while others focus on the dire consequences of honor-shame culture. For each child's protection, we have changed names and identifying details. To spotlight God's presence in their lives, every story ends with a "Light in the Darkness" section recalling our focus to the hope of Jesus Christ.

Throughout Scripture, we see God graciously move through believers by the power of the Holy Spirit to minister in places of profound brokenness. We pray that He does the same through this book. As the global Church confidently and courageously engages with these stories, we pray that all of God's people come away better equipped to both pray and act on behalf of the voiceless and witness the Lord's redeeming work in their lives.

Genesis 1:27 tells us that God created every child in His image. They are precious and valuable in His sight. Scripture also tells us that He desires for all of them to come to saving faith in Christ, who suffered, died, and rose again to pay the penalty for sin so that all who believe in Him would be reconciled to the Father and have eternal life.

So, as you engage with the following stories, we invite you to take a compassionate look at these children and their communities. We invite you to reflect on what you read. Lastly, but most importantly, we invite you to prayerfully ask yourself: *What might the Lord do through the life of this child? What does God's grace look like through their eyes?*

1

AMIR
أمير

Amir watched as his mother rose to her tiptoes and removed the wooden cross hanging in their living room. She then began to wrap it carefully in newspaper.

"I don't want to move," he told her with crossed arms.

He knew it would not make a difference, but he needed to say the truth out loud.

Zoya set her packing items aside and walked toward her son. Gathering him in her arms, she gently placed a kiss on his cheek.

"Your grandfather wants his only grandson closer, in his home country," she said to comfort him, Amir knew, though he sensed the slight edge her words held.

"But this *is* our home country," Amir replied, a pout forming on his lips.

He only knew his grandfather by an old photograph sitting in his father's home office. It lived on a shelf beside history textbooks and journals from his father's recently completed Ph.D. program, as if the patriarch sat looking down on his son's studies with pride. Amir wondered for a brief moment how his grandfather might look upon him and his future accomplishments.

3

From a handful of stories his father, Nasir, often told over dinner, Amir only knew three things about his grandfather: he wielded great power in his father's home country as a judge; no one could argue with him, not even his son; and Amir held the blessing of being his only grandson.

Amir had to admit that his grandfather piqued his curiosity. He wanted to meet the man who produced such fear and reverence in his father. But the desire to meet him was not strong enough to override his reluctance to leave. Amir and his parents had lived in the same town on the same street in the same apartment for his entire life.

How will I make friends? What if Grandfather doesn't like me? What if Baba changes around him?

These questions, among many others, crowded Amir's mind, causing his shoulders to slump with worry. Meanwhile, his mother had resumed packing the wrapped cross into a dusty suitcase. Amir did not understand why she bothered to take it. Their family didn't talk about God.

Amir knew that his mother had grown up Catholic, his baba Muslim. Neither had ever seemed bothered by this difference. Amir could recall only one conversation in which his parents discussed it. They had warned him that other people might take issue with their marriage since they came from different religious backgrounds, and because of this, Amir should keep the subject to himself. But in practice, their faiths looked very similar to Amir. While Zoya occasionally took her son to a church down the road from their apartment, he could not remember the last time they attended a service. His father occasionally went to a nearby mosque, but he did not invite Amir to join him.

Zoya paused in her flurried packing, suddenly appearing lost in thought. Amir glanced up from his own thoughts, startled to see his mother so still. A deep crease had formed between her eyes—something worried her. But before he could ask what, her eyes flew open, and she resumed her task.

TAKEN

Within days, the family said goodbye to everyone they had ever known in their town and began the drive deep into Nasir's home country. Amir pictured his father at his age, roaming through the tall, unkempt grass that lined the roadside as they drew closer to their destination. This country, though not so very different from theirs, had none of the sights or smells Amir anticipated from his father's stories at dinner the night before. Traces of his descriptions remained: tall mountains made purple by the sunset, a sea breeze that swept across your face as you drove through various villages. But the buildings themselves bore signs of decay, abandonment, or—Amir glimpsed bullet holes in the sides of some—*war*.

I do not want to call this home. This place feels wrong, and I don't want to be here.

But almost half an hour later, Amir and his parents arrived at their new apartment down the street from his grandfather's home. Immediately upon their arrival, Amir sensed a tension between his mother and father.

"We must go to the store to get groceries," Zoya said.

"We should visit my father first," Nasir replied.

Their faces drained of color. Amir wondered why they had come.

Within a week, the tension between his parents had intensified to the point of worrying Amir.

One night, he overheard his father speaking to his mother in a hushed, firm tone, saying, "My family name, my heritage, is descended from Mohammed. Do you know what this means? The stakes are much higher. The shame is much greater!"

In a shaking voice, Amir heard his mother respond, "What do we do?"

He did not know what his parents meant by this, but Amir felt fear growing inside of him with each word. One night after dinner, to break the long silence that filled the room in the absence of his father's stories, Amir decided to ask his parents what troubled them.

As he rose from the table with a stack of dirty plates, the question ready on his lips, he heard the screeching of several vehicles outside their building, the stomping of many pairs of boots, and then the forceful crack of their front door bursting open. It flew off its hinges and crashed against the entryway table.

A group of five or six men poured into the house, shouting, guns leveled at Amir and his family.

Three men grabbed Nasir, forcing him to his knees, while Zoya's cries mingled with the shouting. One of the men struck her and hauled her out into the hall. She screamed even louder, this time for Amir, and before one of the men could grab him, he ran into his mother's arms.

ABANDONED

These men are so full of anger and hate. I can't believe they spat at Mama when they dragged her to the car. What do they want? Where did they take Baba? Why did they do this to us?

Amir and his mother clung to each other, peering into the dark of their new surroundings. He saw in his mind over and over a picture of the men dragging his father into a waiting truck outside their home. Amid their shouting, Amir had made out the word "infidel" several times. Muslims referred to Christians as infidels, Amir knew. But his father practiced Islam.

After the men drove away with his father, the group who took Amir and Zoya shoved them into a separate truck. It arrived at a decrepit, empty house somewhere in the city. The men pushed them inside the house, then into a back room with nothing but a stained mattress on the floor.

"Oh, God, help us," Zoya whispered hoarsely.

Amir and his mother remained in the musty room together for what seemed like two weeks before the radicals—*ISIS*, Amir knew—disrupted his life again. One night, as mother and son ate cold bread together on the shared mattress, the men burst in and summoned Zoya to follow them. She glanced at Amir, that deep crease between her eyebrows returning, and stood to follow them.

Unsure of what to make of this, Amir settled back onto the mattress and picked at what remained of the loaf. After a while, he laid on his back and listened to the sounds outside the door. Voices, the scrape of chairs, shouts, cars passing outside, a horn.

He did not hear his mother.

Feeling alone and without hope, Amir wept as softly as he could, only daring to voice his desperation in his mind. Whom he pleaded with, he did not know.

Help me. Please, rescue me. I'm so afraid. I'm alone. She's left me alone. I don't know what to do. Help me be strong. Send help. Please.

REUNITED

Two months went by. Amir knew this because he had overheard one of the men say the day's date. He had long passed feeling shocked, but his devastation at not knowing what happened to his mother remained. He did not know how to find her again, and this thought filled Amir with anxiety. It did not help that the men had moved him to a different house at some point in those two months, though it looked the same as the first—dark, unfamiliar, and absent of hope. Amir counted the paint cracks on the wall, trying to find something to focus his thoughts on to hold back the panic he had come to know so well in his shadowy prison.

Suddenly, he heard a familiar noise. The door burst open, and the light that streamed in through the hall made him squint.

When his vision settled, Amir cried out, "Mama!"

Zoya ran toward her son, tears streaming down her face and onto his shoulder as she embraced him so tightly he couldn't breathe. Amir drew back to see his mother's face, still contorted with fear.

One of the men, his voice more distinct than the others due to its gruffness, shouted at Zoya: "You've seen him! Now, go! Bring back the money or we will kill him."

Amir had thought she had abandoned him, but now he understood she had no choice. As the man raised his gun and pointed it directly at Amir's face, Zoya kissed his forehead, her lips trembling, and turned to leave again. Before Amir could stop her, his mother had vanished and the man with the gruff voice had slammed the door shut.

RESCUED

Zoya stumbled from the house and down the steep, paved road, frantically searching for help. At that moment, a taxi pulled up next to her, and the driver offered her a ride.

"Where to?" he asked as Zoya climbed into the backseat.

"My son, they have my son! They're going to kill him if I don't bring money back. I need help! Please, help me!"

The driver hit his brakes and gaped at Zoya from the rearview mirror.

"Get out. I don't want any trouble," he said with a tinge of fear, eyes darting to his rearview mirror to assure himself they had not been followed.

Zoya cried bitterly as she stepped from the car onto the side of the road. She held her face in her hands, not wanting to watch the car drive away and the last of her hope with it. But after a few moments, she heard tires approaching again.

Glancing up, Zoya saw the same taxi, the same driver, as before. He motioned nervously for her to get in again.

"You do not wear a hijab. Are you Christian?" the man asked.

She nodded eagerly.

"I will take you somewhere," he said. "Tell them you are Christian. They will help you."

After many stops and turns, the driver finally pulled up to a large metal gate, and without a word, directed Zoya to get out. Warily inching closer to the gate, she took a breath and rang the buzzer. When a face appeared, she pulled out her small wallet, which she had kept hidden for months in an inside pocket in her skirt, and held up a worn picture of Jesus.

"I need help. Please, they have my son."

The face across the gate looked her over. Then, the gate shuddered open. Half a dozen American soldiers greeted her on the other side.

FREEDOM

Back at the house with his captors, Amir laid on his side on the mattress, hugging his knees. His body ached with the stiffness of being immobile all day. He thought of finally standing in order to stretch his limbs when he heard a series of shouts. They reminded him of the last time he saw his home, of the men who came bursting through his door. But this time, the voices shouted in English, not Arabic.

Amir sprung up from the floor. As he ran toward the door, it flew open, and a man in uniform scanned the room, searching. When he locked eyes on Amir, Amir knew that the man was looking for him. Before Amir could decide if he should be worried or elated, the soldier grabbed him and passed him to another waiting soldier, who moved him quickly through the hall.

The Americans passed Amir from one soldier to the next like a prized baton. Suddenly, Amir found himself at the front of the house, peering down at the dark, menacing faces of the ISIS radicals. They now sat on their knees with their hands tied behind them.

They glared at Amir, hatred emanating from their eyes.

But then he felt himself carried past them and into the passenger seat of a waiting vehicle, where his mother immediately enveloped him in a hug.

I am free.

LIGHT IN THE DARKNESS

In a 2017 report by HOSTAGE US, conflict and lack of a single state authority within Syria, Iraq, and Yemen has created an environment ripe for kidnapping, with one of the most prominent actors being the Islamic State group (IS).[1] Marriage between Muslims and Christians is forbidden in many countries within the Middle East, and Nasir's choice to marry a Catholic ultimately brought shame to his family's name and made him a target for radicals. *How is God working in the midst of this challenge?* Amid their fear, shame, and persecution, Amir and his mother clung to the hope that someone, even God, might free them. For the rest of her life, Zoya would not forget that Jesus gave her common ground with the soldiers. Her reminder of this hope, this Savior, in the form of a picture kept in her wallet ultimately moved the American soldiers to help her free Amir.

*The hand of our God is for good on all who seek him, and the power of his wrath is against all who forsake him. - **Ezra 8:22b***

2

INAYA
عناية

The air was heavy, like a thick cloud Inaya waded through as she walked to her bed. She could feel it hanging off her skin, along with the myriad of smells that made up their home, this camp for the forgotten. Some days in this place felt harder than others. When the weather grew warm, the air and the smells, and the noise seemed unbearable. In those moments, Inaya could feel the collective weight of all her neighbors' hopelessness. She felt it on herself, too.

Refugee, they say. *Muslim refugee.* Muslim, *yes. This is true. But* refugee? *I don't understand why this country calls us that or why we had to come here in the first place. I have no memories of my birth country. Now, my name,* Inaya, *matters little and* refugee *matters most. I have known since 3 years old, my age when we came here, that I don't matter. Because I am* Muslim *and a* refugee *and a girl.*

As Inaya climbed onto the rug her mother laid out for her each night to sleep on, she tried to shut off her thoughts. But like the foul air in their tent, they clung to her. To live as a refugee, especially as a girl, felt to Inaya the worst life Allah could ordain. For years, she had wrestled with the impression that she and the other girls in the camp did not matter as much as the boys did. She watched as the adults did not listen to the girls, did not pay as much attention to them, as they did the boys. The more Inaya thought about this, the more it saddened her. Her heart, naturally compassionate toward others, overflowed with grief for all the daughters of the camp who, like her, believed their lives held little value.

Yet, her parents had recently surprised her by allowing her to attend a nearby school—a Christian school, taught by *infidels*, as she had heard the adults in her community call them. Unlike any other school in the area, this Christian school accepted refugee students. Inaya hoped that her parents valued her future enough to continue to overlook the school's religious teachings and let her learn there, a place where she might finally belong.

As her eyelids grew heavy, Inaya drifted off to sleep, grateful for what tomorrow would bring: her first day at school.

CHRISTIAN SCHOOL

Inaya awoke with anticipation. She wanted to get to the school as soon as possible in case her parents changed their minds about letting her learn from the Christians. She figured they would cover the basics of education —math, reading, writing—but would they teach her about the infidel religion, too? Surprisingly, the idea did not unsettle Inaya, but made her curious. She shouldered the small bag her mother had given her, packed with an extra scarf and some dried fruit, and stepped out of their tent with a racing heart.

As she approached the gated, white building, Inaya saw a crowd of children at the entrance. Two teachers stood near the doorway to welcome the students. She tentatively glanced at the teacher closest to her and risked a smile; Inaya wore a hijab and did not know how the school might respond. Considering this, she hesitated. But the teacher simply beamed at Inaya and said, "Welcome! How wonderful to see you!"

Inaya believed her.

Two other teachers greeted Inaya in the same way—as if her arrival truly brought them joy. Inaya had never experienced this kind of welcome, not from anyone in the camp, not from anyone in the city, and definitely not from strangers. Throughout her day of classes, she marveled at the teachers' attitude toward her. Did they not know that she bowed to Allah and that she lived in a refugee camp? Why did they show her such kindness?

On her walk back to the camp, Inaya practiced what she might say when asked about her day at school.

My teachers show me love, such happiness because I came! They make me feel like I matter to them. Today, during one of our lessons, a teacher told me about the prophet Jesus, but she called him God. She also said God made me "in His image," as if I look like Him, as if He made me a girl on purpose, for a purpose. My teacher even prayed for me—not like we pray to Allah, but like Jesus sat right next to us, listening. Mama, I love the school. I love the way they pray. I cannot wait to go back tomorrow!

Inaya reentered the camp, navigating the narrow walkways between its various dwellings until she came upon her family's tent. Setting her bag down in the corner, she picked up her baby sister from her mother's lap. As much as she longed to, she knew that she could not share these thoughts with her mother, her father...or anyone.

A FATHER'S CHOICE

After a month at the Christian school, Inaya could feel a change inside of her. Through their affection, prayers, and lessons about Jesus, her teachers demonstrated to Inaya what the Christians had that she and her family did not—faith in a God who abounded in love. She adored them and the school and secretly began to open their sacred book, the Bible, which her teachers had offered to her to read.

As Inaya walked home from school one day, she remembered a verse her teachers taught that morning. The words moved through her mind like rippling water: *"I am the way and the truth and the life. No one comes to the Father except through me."* But the warmth of the words faded away as she walked into her family's tent and felt an overwhelming dread.

Her baba's face had changed since that morning. His dark eyes strained against the dim light, while his mouth hung grimly from his face like a lopsided moon. Inaya felt a heavy pit in her stomach. Her mother sat next to him, tears staining her face. She pleaded with her husband.

"Please, Youssef. Please," she begged.

But his face only hardened the more she cried. He had made a decision, Inaya knew, and he would not sway from it. But why did he look so determinedly at *her*?

"Inaya," he began. "You will marry."

Another wail filled the tent. Inaya did not know if it came from her mother or from her own lips.

"We have two proposals for you," her father continued. "As Allah wills, one of them will take you as their wife next month."

He spoke as if informing her she needed to watch her siblings or pick up after herself in the tent.

Married?

"Good options, both of them," her father continued. "One from a man your grandfather has worked closely with before. Though older, he has great wealth and will take care of you. The other comes from your cousin, Ibrahim."

Ibrahim, "the radical," her family called him. A member of ISIS, they never spoke of him.

"No," Inaya heard herself whisper.

At that moment, she remembered a conversation she had recently overheard between her parents. One night, when they thought she and her siblings slept, her baba had told her mother they could not keep going like this with so many mouths to feed. Though the local resource center for refugees supplied food and sanitary items, the packages could not sustain their large family. He had to do something. After years of desperate hunger and suffering the camp's diseases, he had no hope of an alternative.

Inaya thought he meant that they would leave the camp. Not that he would marry her to a stranger.

I know I must honor my family and obey. But why should my life carry so much burden? I have tried not to eat too much, to stay out of the way, to help where I can. Why must I do this unspeakable thing? To think of leaving my family to marry one of these men!

Panic and anger rose within Inaya like two intertwining clouds of ash. She did not know how to be someone's wife. The decisions that would make up the rest of her life did not belong to her. She wanted to scream with rage, start pleading like her mother. But she knew it would make no difference, as it had made no difference when her mother spoke. Here, in this place, her voice did not matter.

But it did at school.

Even if she could not say the words out loud, Inaya believed that her teachers would hear her, that they would somehow know she needed help. If their Jesus remained close to the brokenhearted, as she had heard them say once, then maybe their God might help her, too.

Tomorrow, I will ask my teachers at the school for help. I have seen them praying to their God. I have prayed with them. If hope for me exists, it lives there, with them.

That night, Inaya curled up on her mat and prayed, over and over, in the name of Jesus, their Savior. She prayed that He would save her, too.

A DESPERATE PRAYER

As Inaya approached the school building the next day, her teachers Mr. Aaban and Ms. Fattah stood at the entrance, greeting the children by name as they usually did. Inaya passed by them and heard their bright, cheerful greeting, "Sabah-l-khayr, Inaya." She knew that she should say in return, "Sabah-n-nur," but the words would not leave her stiff lips.

Inaya wanted to speak but did not know how to start. In shame, she cast her face down, quickly moving inside the school to avoid her teachers' eyes. Tears threatened to cascade down her cheeks as her teachers looked on, concern spreading over their faces.

After her first class, Inaya stepped into the hallway to risk another prayer to Jesus. If not to take away the two marriage proposals, then to at least help her get through the school day without crying like a baby in front of everyone. But before she could pray, Ms. Fattah approached her.

"Inaya, why do you seem so sad?"

At the compassion in Ms. Fattah's voice, Inaya broke down in tears.

Ms. Fattah and Mr. Aaban took Inaya to their offices so she could speak with them uninterrupted. But even in the private space, she could barely utter the words.

"I must do an unspeakable thing," Inaya finally said. "Baba says I must marry. We don't have enough food, enough medicine, enough *anything*. I must lessen our burden and bring honor to my family by marrying one of the men who have made proposals to my father. But I do not want to."

Inaya tilted her chin up just enough to see the expressions on Ms. Fattah and Mr. Aaban's faces. Their smiles faded the more she shared, and when she had finished, a deep sense of grief silenced all three of them.

After several moments, Ms. Fattah whispered, "Let us bring this to Jesus. He hears our prayers, Inaya."

Inaya exhaled. They had suggested the very thing she wanted to do.

You say you are the Way, the Truth, and the Life, Jesus. I want to believe this, to believe in you. Please, help me.

Ms. Fattah and Mr. Aaban prayed over Inaya, asking Jesus to intervene and close the doors to both men so that a marriage to either of them would not happen. They prayed for God to make a way for Inaya to stay in school, continue her education, and grow in the wisdom and love of the Lord. As their words settled over her, Inaya's fear began to ease bit by bit. When they finished praying, she thanked her teachers for listening to her and for making her feel safe. She thanked them, too, for introducing her to Jesus.

THE WAY FORWARD

Every day afterward, Inaya arrived at school early to pray with Ms. Fattah and Mr. Aaban. The two young teachers prayed to Jesus on Inaya's behalf, pleading with Him to help her and direct the course of her life. These prayers buoyed Inaya's spirit so much that she felt herself becoming something—someone—different. She believed that this new Inaya had everything to do with Jesus.

Five days after Inaya and her teachers began praying, Inaya walked into her family's tent, and the horrible dread she felt before returned to her in a crippling rush. But this time, Inaya knew that she did not need to fear. As peace settled over her, she noticed her mother smiling.

Her baba resignedly told her the news: a marriage would not go forward. Both of the proposals fell through—the older man suspiciously stopped answering his phone, and Ibrahim, who lived in their old country, could no longer get to them because the border had closed. Inaya would remain with her family and continue her education at the Christian school.

Inaya could hardly believe it. Tears and more tears sprang from her eyes as she flew into her mother's open arms. She felt overcome with gratitude and an increasingly fervent belief that Jesus—*"the way and the truth and the life"*—had answered her prayers.

I worship you, Jesus. I worship you! You have helped me, saved me. You really are my God, my Savior.

The following morning, Ms. Fattah and Mr. Aaban could not believe the sight of the joyous girl running toward them. Beaming with delight and wonder, she cried out before she reached their embrace, "Jesus heard! Jesus heard! He closed the doors! He closed them!"

The words tumbled out of her so rapidly that her teachers could not help but laugh. Inaya then shared how she wanted to continue learning in order to be a lawyer one day, a lawyer who helped other refugee girls just like her. Girls who have no voice, no hope, no truth.

"I want to know Jesus. I want *so much* to know this Jesus," she said.

LIGHT IN THE DARKNESS

UNICEF reported in 2022 that 700,000 girls are forced into child marriage in the MENA region each year, and interrupted education and school closures increase the risk of child marriage by 22%.[2] *How is God working in the midst of this challenge?* Ananias House has witnessed how Christian schools open new pathways for children living in refugee camps by offering an opportunity to receive an education and hear the gospel of Jesus Christ. Inaya's access to this Christian school allowed her, a young Muslim, to observe men and women who had given their lives to Jesus. Her teachers educated *and* discipled each of the children who attended their school by demonstrating their own dependence on Jesus and the transformative power of His love. Through this discipleship model, they built relationships that strengthened the refugee community. Inaya could now pass on her new hope to those around her.

Ask and it will be given to you; seek, and you will find; knock, and it will be opened to you. For everyone who asks receives, and the one who seeks finds, and to the one who knocks it will be opened. - **Matthew 7:7-8**

3

JALAL
جلال

"ISIS! ISIS is coming! They are here!"

Jalal couldn't move. A chilling terror pinned him to his bed. He tried to open his eyes, but open or closed, he saw only darkness.

ISIS.

He watched in his mind's eye the frantic hands of parents grabbing their children, of women trying to hide behind cars, of moonlight that appeared mottled as it reflected off of the storefront windows onto black cement streets. He heard the crackle of gunshots echoing through their village, followed by long, mournful wails.

"Mama, Baba, run! We have to run!"

The sound of his own voice awoke him. With the words still hanging from his lips, Jalal knew his screams had reverberated on this side of the nightmare as well. He sat up. When the pulse in his eardrums lessened, he heard another, softer sound. Its familiarity brought tears to his eyes.

"Shh...you are safe, habibi. You are safe."

Mama!

Jalal reached out for his mother in the darkness, and she quickly came to sit beside him on the bed. Covering his shivering body with her warm arms, she held him close and tried to soothe the images away. Jalal knit his fingers through her hair where it fell behind her back and closed his eyes as she rocked back and forth.

His bedroom brightened with her there. Even the moon outside of his window, now clear in the night sky, streamed its light through the bedroom, chasing away the shadows.

"Mama?" he asked hoarsely.

His tears had left a wet mark on her pajama shirt. She continued to rock back and forth.

"Yes, my Jalal?"

But he thought better of voicing his fears. At his age, he believed that nightmares should no longer make him afraid. And yet his mother came to his bedroom at least once a week to comfort him.

ISIS had invaded their village many years before. The memories of the radical group kidnapping and recruiting and killing neighbors and friends tormented Jalal's mind like a persistent migraine. To lose so many so quickly had devastated him, his mother knew. Boys he played soccer with, girls who frequented their apartment to play with Jalal's sister—all gone within a day, within hours.

When the men came, their massive guns slung over their shoulders, Jalal had hidden with his mother and one of his sisters behind a shot-out delivery truck parked along the street. His baba grabbed his other sister, falling to the ground and pulling the dead body of a neighbor on top of them as a would-be shield.

Jalal hated himself for remembering these things and for letting the memories impact him the way they did.

What a baby—why do I cry like this all the time? Why does Mama have to come and hold me for me to stop seeing the bad things? I just want to forget.

In the years since ISIS invaded their village, Jalal watched people slowly rebuild the community. But the absence of so many loved ones cast a shadow over all of their daily lives. He could feel their loss as he walked past the souq, the school, the cafes and gas stations and shops, and the churches most of all. Many people in the village left flickering candles in glass cylinders outside the nearest church each month, every time stopping short of venturing in. Jalal's family did this, as did their remaining neighbors.

But what if ISIS came again?

The thought petrified Jalal, so much so that his breathing grew quick and shallow. His mother hugged him tighter. But Jalal gently disentangled himself from her arms, opting instead to burrow his face in his pillow, away from his mother, away from the moonlight streaming in through the window, away from his shameful fears.

He needed to prove his strength to his mother, to his sisters, to his father. Most of all, he needed to prove that he could help should ISIS come again.

THE VISITORS

Though Christian, Jalal and his family had not attended their church in years, not since ISIS came. So it surprised Jalal when Mrs. Jeena and Ms. Najat from church came for a visit. The two ladies looked the same— brown hair cut short above their shoulders, colorful clothes, several lines flecked around their eyes and mouth from the many smiles they dealt out like candy. They offered Jalal one of these smiles after greeting his mother with a tight hug and kisses on both cheeks.

"Thank you for inviting us," Ms. Najat said.

Jalal's jaw dropped: *his mother had invited them to come to their home!* She had not invited anyone to do that since before ISIS.

His mother ushered the women into their sitting room, where all three of them settled down on the patterned cushions on the floor. On their wooden coffee table sat a steaming tea kettle atop a silver tray with three glass tea cups, some milk, and a small dish of dried apricots. Jalal could not remember seeing these items before and blinked back his surprise.

He took in the scene before him—the glittering tray on the coffee table and the brightly dressed ladies around it, the drapes thrown back from the only window in that part of their home—and wondered if he had fallen asleep again without knowing. But this dream did not frighten him.

"How are you, Hamsa?" Mrs. Jeena asked.

Jalal's mother glanced in the direction of his bedroom, where he had hidden himself from view.

"I will not lie. It has not been easy."

The three women spoke quietly over tea for a very long time, what felt to Jalal like several hours. After his mother's response to Mrs. Jeena, Jalal could no longer hear their conversation, just the gentle tone of their voices creating a soothing rhythm, like melodies overlapping in a song he knew from childhood.

At one point, he left his hiding place, crept along the hallway, and peered around the corner to see Ms. Najat reaching for her purse, where she retrieved a blue, tattered Bible. She opened it and set it in front of them on the coffee table, the tea tray pushed to the side. Together, they read several verses. Then, they prayed.

When Mrs. Jeena and Ms. Najat left that afternoon, Jalal saw tears in his mother's eyes, though she smiled, too. In that small span of time, much about her had changed, he realized. She had brushed her hair back from her face, where it usually hung loose and tangled. Her hands, which usually shook, moved quickly and delicately across the coffee table, placing their tea items on the tray to bring back to the kitchen.

After several moments, Hamsa saw her son standing in the hallway watching her. Instead of chiding him for lurking in the hall and instructing him to go do his homework, she simply smiled again. For the first time in a long time, Jalal noticed that her smile reached her eyes.

THE WORD

As night approached, Jalal could almost taste the familiar dread creeping over him again. His stomach churned with it. He laid his head down on his pillow and repeated the same thought over and over in his mind.

I don't want to go to sleep. I don't want to go to sleep. I don't want to go to sleep.

He tried to fight the inevitable by counting the stars visible beyond his window, anything to distract himself from the nightmare awaiting him. He rolled onto his stomach, clutching the pillow beneath his head as if to anchor himself to the waking world.

Suddenly, he heard his bedroom door creak open. As if sensing his restlessness, his mother walked into the room. She sat on his bed and placed her hand on Jalal's back. From the sound of her voice, he could tell she stared not at him, but out of the window.

"Terrible things have happened in our community, habibi. I know they haunt your dreams. I will not lie to you and tell you that bad things will not happen again, but I can tell you a few things about God."

She paused for what seemed like several minutes. Jalal felt the weight of sleep on his eyelids, but he wanted to hear what she said next.

"He is good. He is powerful. He is in charge of everything. He hears our prayers. He loves us. He saw us through our hard times before, and He is still with us. *He is still with us*, Jalal."

Jalal rolled onto his side, toward her honeyed voice. She glanced down at him, the moonlight revealing the softness in her face. Then, she pulled from behind her a dark, heavy object and placed it carefully by his pillow. Sitting up on his elbows, Jalal scrutinized it. The Arabic letters on its cover shone like whorls of gold. His mother's Bible.

"Together, let's focus on God instead of fear. Perfect love casts out fear."

For several weeks afterward, Jalal and his mother dedicated an hour each night before bed to reading the Bible together. As they did, Jalal's nightmares tormented him less and less, slowly losing their power. Then, one day, Jalal opened his eyes after a quiet, peaceful sleep and realized the nightmares had not come.

Their study of Scripture impacted Jalal's waking hours, too. Where he had fallen behind in school, he began to catch up, and his teachers commended his newfound joy and excitement about learning. Jalal's mother recognized this change as having come from their time in the Word, so she asked her husband if they could return to church.

At their first church service in over five years, Jalal and his family entered the building together without fear. Filing into a pew at the back of the chapel, they opened their Bibles, ready to receive God's teaching. Glancing down at the page, Jalal whispered to himself the first verse to catch his eye:

"The LORD is my light and my salvation; whom shall I fear? The LORD is the stronghold of my life; of whom shall I be afraid?"

LIGHT IN THE DARKNESS

In 2022, the National Library of Medicine reported that 35-40% of Syrian children in Turkïye and Syria are estimated to be experiencing PTSD symptoms.[3] The scarcity of mental health resources along with ongoing trauma from both economic conditions and radical groups make their situations even more complex. Jalal's nightmares stemmed from unhealed trauma from several years before. To make matters worse, his family made a practice of isolating themselves from other believers due to the risk of gathering. *How is God working in the midst of this challenge?* As Jalal's mother sought out community again, she and her family entered into a support network vital to their spiritual health and development. Communion with God through His Word and sharing grief and trauma with other believers lead many Christians across the MENA region down paths of healing.

God is our refuge and strength, a very present help in trouble. - **Psalm 46:1**

4

RIHAB
رحاب

In their third-floor apartment, Rihab sat motionless on her bed, silenced by the cost of her decision. The daily cacophony of revved engines, street conversations, and wind-rustled palm leaves rose up from her window, but the deafening voice in her mind eclipsed them all: *Is this Christian God worth your life?*

Her heart resounded: *Yes.*

At sunset, the call to prayer beckoned those faithful to Mohammed to unfold their prayer mats. For the first time in her life, Rihab did not heed it, surprised to find that where panic should have settled in her heart, she felt only peace. Where guilt should have imprisoned her inner being, she only felt her soul's sense of freedom. These she took as testimonies of the Lord's faithfulness. From this moment on, she would never again bow her knees to Allah and his falsehoods. Instead, she would live for the true God, the God of all Creation who took on the role of a servant out of love for His people. She could not believe she had lived so long without Him.

"Jesus."

She spoke His name into the silence. Even saying it felt surreal to Rihab. His name had changed everything. It had expelled the lies she believed for so long and had awakened her to a new, fresh hope. *Jesus*: the name of the One who truly loved her.

"Forgive me, Lord. And please, take my life. Take my heart. Take me. I want to walk with you forever."

Only she and God could hear this conversation. Rihab found solace in this fact; it allowed her to linger in the peace of the moment, staving off what would soon come. She new that once she opened her bedroom door and rejoined her family, nothing could remain the same.

THE BETRAYAL

I have not told Mama and Baba, or even Haman. I fear they will hate me, that they will feel the shame of my decision or prevent me from going. But I must leave this place. They might kill me if they discover I have given my life to Jesus! I must go. I have made a friend in the United States, and she can help me get there.

Rihab placed her pen in the open journal to mark her spot and closed the book. Since the moment she had given her life to Jesus, she had begun journaling her thoughts and questions, as well as the path she believed the Lord laid out before her. She felt that He had provided a way out: she had connected with a believer online who had shared the gospel with her. As she had gotten to know this girl and her family from across the ocean, it became apparent that they would provide a safe place to flee to in the aftermath of her conversion.

Though she had recently turned 18, Rihab's father still held authority over the major decisions of her life. Rihab knew he could never allow her to live out her faith openly, so despite how much it frightened her to leave her parents and brother, she had to go. A daughter could do nothing worse to a good, Muslim family than to denounce Mohammed, let alone for the prophet Jesus. But Rihab knew the truth now: far more than a prophet, Jesus, the Son of God, the Savior of the world, died for her sins.

She suspected her father knew she believed this now, too.

Over the last month, he had started acting strangely, questioning Rihab about what she did in her room, who she spoke to as she prayed, what secrets she hid from him.

But none of this could stop her from opening God's Word and receiving the comfort her Heavenly Father offered there. She held the Bible in her hand, a gift she had received from the Christian church around the corner from her house. She had snuck in one afternoon on her way home from the bakery just to see what it felt like inside. The face of the sweet woman who had greeted her flashed in her mind, and she smiled. They had only spoken for a few moments, but in that time, Rihab felt a sense of belonging.

With her bedroom door cracked so she could smell the aroma of her mother's spiced lamb and baba ganoush, Rihab climbed atop her bed, pulled the small Bible out from under her pillow where she hid it, and began to read Psalm 1.

Whispering the words out loud in uncertain English, she read, *"Blessed is the one who does not walk in step with the wicked or stand in the way that sinners take or sit in the company of mockers, but whose delight is in the law of the Lord, and who meditates on his law day and night."*

The creak of her bedroom door startled Rihab from her reading. Her father walked across its threshold, rage in his eyes.

"What are you reading?" he cried, plucking the Bible from her trembling hands to examine it.

Rihab prayed in her mind, a voiceless plea to her Father in heaven.

Please help me.

THE DEPARTURE

A week later, Rihab could not recognize her life. Every day, her baba raged at her deception, her betrayal, her shameful act which threatened to ruin the entire family's reputation. Even her mother had changed; she refused to meet Rihab's gaze, and the few times she did, Rihab shrunk back from the disappointment in her eyes.

Yet amid their constant shaming, Rihab turned her eyes to her Savior, reminding herself that her parents did not yet know the saving truth of Jesus Christ.

How can they know the wonder of this faith when Islam still holds them captive?

Despite her desire to trust in Jesus no matter what, fear had made itself

Rihab's constant companion. She knew that her father remained within his rights to kill her for her conversion to Christianity. She had heard stories of this taking place in other families. For a long time, there had existed among their people an unseen understanding that "honor killings" restored to the family the honor their wayward family member had stolen.

Rihab knew she had to leave so as not to give her father an opportunity to take her life—a life she now desperately wanted to live for Jesus. Yet she hesitated at the thought of leaving Haman.

Her brother had not followed Islam in the same way her parents did. So, one day, when visiting his house, just two streets away from their family's home, Rihab told Haman of her newfound faith in Jesus and her commitment to follow Him. Rihab told him about her friend who lived in America, and how this friend had prepared a place for her where she could live safely among other Christians and freely worship the Lord.

"I do not understand, and I do not think it wise that you leave on your own, but I fear what Baba will do to you if you do not go," Haman had said with deep sorrow in his eyes.

Upon leaving his home that day, Rihab promised her brother that she would go to him first before she left for good. Haman's words, returning to her mind, gave Rihab enough strength to gather the supplies she had hidden in an old suitcase in her closet for her eventual escape. She took the suitcase in one hand and pulled her Bible out from under her pillow, which she had dug out of the trash and hid away again without her father's knowledge. Glancing one last time around her room, she slipped quietly out of the door.

THE OFFERING

Rihab stepped into the street, covering her head and trying not to draw attention to herself as she walked the few miles to Haman's home. As the distance grew between her and her father, she began to feel lighter—the oppressive, daily weight upon her chest easing bit by bit. The sun lowered into the early evening sky and tears rippled down her cheeks in relief.

As she turned the corner, she spotted the small church that stood on the left side of the road ahead. It was the same one Rihab had entered weeks before, where a sweet woman had gifted her a Bible. Adjusting her suitcase in her hand and clutching her Bible with the other, she took a deep breath and slipped in unnoticed. After all that the Lord had done for her, she desired to leave an offering in thanks.

No one greeted her at the door like before, which Rihab found herself grateful for. Wanting to be alone with God, she sat in the back of the room designated for worship. She closed her eyes and prayed to the Lord, heaping up her gratitude for the comfort of the Holy Spirit and her assurance that He remained with her. In that moment, she knew in her heart that He would never leave her, no matter what she faced.

The sun seeping through the church windows retreated. Just like the moment in her bedroom when she committed to follow Jesus, Rihab desired to linger. She did not want to think about what might come next. But she knew she must hurry, that although she sat in her Father's house, she must flee. Taking up her bag again, she left several coins in the offering box and pulled open the door to leave.

Suddenly, Rihab lost her vision. Blinking against an onslaught of lights —flashlights—she tried to see in front of her.

Shurta! Police.

All at once, the men in uniform came toward her. Rihab could not speak for all the questions in her mind.

The police! Did Baba call them? I was only here for a few moments. I don't understand how they knew I was here. Did they find the conversations on my computer, the ones talking about the gospel, about my plans to join my friend in America? I can't imagine what they will do to me. Will I die tonight? Lord, please help me!

Strong hands pulled at her arms, now shaking, and dragged her to a waiting vehicle.

THE DARKNESS

A guard threw Rihab onto the cell's dirt floor, which smelled so foul that she almost vomited. Her chin painfully hit the ground. As she moved to sit up, she tried to unpin one of her arms from beneath her to wipe the filth from her face, but someone forcefully flipped her over before she could.

Now laid back on her elbows, Rihab stared at the face of the guard who had tossed her there. She knew by his expression what he intended to do, and she knew no one would stop him.

THE SONG

Sometime later, Rihab heard her cell door click shut. A metallic smell mingled with the cell's putrid air as a sob fell from her lips.

Jesus. Jesus. Jesus.

She curled into herself in the dark, remembering the church. No matter what she faced, the Lord would not leave her—*this* Rihab believed more than anything else. As thoughts of the Lord filled her mind, a peace filled her spirit, so deep and all-encompassing that Rihab knew He had not left her. He never would.

At this realization, Rihab felt a song begin to well up in her spirit. She had heard it online just a few weeks before and listened to it in secret when her parents left home each week for her brother's house. As the lyrics returned to her, Rihab felt a surge of strength in her body, as if the song, building inside of her, brought with it a remembrance of the peace of God.

Despite the stench and the rough, pebbled ground beneath her, she rose up on her knees. Despite the evil committed against her by her parents, by the police, by this most evil of men—the violent guard outside her cell—Rihab spread her hands above her head, toward God in heaven.

She cleared her throat a few times in order to shakily sing the first verse, now pouring forth from her:

"When peace like a river, attendeth my way, when sorrows like sea billows roll; whatever my lot, Thou hast taught me to say, it is well, it is well, with my soul. It is well with my soul, it is well, it is well, with my soul."

THE DELIVERY

The next morning, Rihab saw between the bars of her cell the man who had violated her the night before. She trembled with fear, clutching her skirt more tightly to her body, but lifted her chin to meet his gaze.

"Released," he said, with an odd smugness.

Praise bubbled from her lips until the nameless man spoke again.

Now she understood him. Greeting her father meant greeting her death.

The guard scoffed, turning away as she cried, "Jesus, *Jesus*, I need you."

A few minutes later, she stepped out of her cell. But when she exited the jail and stumbled onto the street, her father did not greet her.

Haman, her beloved brother, stood before her. When she walked toward him, his face crumbled. With tears in his eyes, he embraced her, and that embrace, so warm and loving, affirmed for Rihab that Jesus intended to protect her from death at her father's hands.

An unutterable gratitude overtook her again. As Rihab clutched her brother tighter, she offered the Lord a silent prayer of thanks.

"Come," Haman said. "We must get you to America, to safety."

LIGHT IN THE DARKNESS

In the MENA region, Sharia-based or Sharia-influenced state laws remain common, and conversion from Islam to Christianity is a violation in many places.* The head of the family holds the right to exact discipline, and this can range from ostracizing the relative to killing them. *How is God working in the midst of this challenge?* Today, those whom God calls to Himself and who live out their faith openly in the MENA region reflect how deeply they consider Him worthy of their devotion. Through the witness of a believer across the world, Rihab learned about Jesus, and His love drew her to give up her life and follow Him. In the darkest of places, she felt His peace comforting her. He did not forsake her. Just as Paul and Silas sang praises to God from their own imprisonment in Acts 16, Rihab lifted up her hands and experienced freedom by worshiping her Father in the confines of her cell.

Let your gentle spirit be known to all people. The Lord is near. Do not be anxious about anything, but in everything by prayer and pleading with thanksgiving let your requests be made known to God. And the peace of God, which surpasses all comprehension, will guard your hearts and minds in Christ Jesus. - **Philippians 4:5-7 (NASB)**

5

ZAYD

زيد

As the sun rose over the soundless tent city, Zayd yawned awake on his mat. It was his favorite hour of the day, when the sunlight stretched across the canvas of their home, emitting warmth and a call to rise. The children in the tents next door had yet to break the morning's silence. Rubbing his eyes with both hands, Zayd sat up and tried to recall what the day held.

He remembered a time when his mornings seemed to fly by with hurried preparation for school, his favorite place. His mother would have to tell him three times to sit down and eat his breakfast before Zayd would slow his eager movements—packing his bag with books, tightening his shoelaces —to greet his plate of za'atar bread and pickled turnips.

Each day at school offered Zayd a new discovery about life, about the world he lived in, and he relished the moments he spent with his teachers, with whom he could ask the many questions that crowded his mind. Though only 5 or 6 then, Zayd still remembered. Their old life came back to him in dreams.

Even if Zayd tried to go back to that school, at 15, he had aged out of it, and no upper level school in the area took refugees as students. The only future left to him involved working alongside his father fixing the cars of the people in town who could afford it. Some spat at Zayd's father when they paid him. Some refused to pay a refugee at all.

As he rose from his mat, Zayd saw his baba welcome someone strangely familiar into their tent. He had seen the man before, a Christian who often came into their community to talk among the families. Zayd had watched him, curious at how the man went from tent to tent praying with families, always smiling. He looked like one of them—like a faithful Muslim—but he did not pray to Allah.

His baba had taught Zayd that infidels would end up in *Jahannam* when they left this life. The thought of this smiling man in hell made Zayd feel strangely sad.

His father motioned for the man to sit down. Zayd could barely hide the shock from his face. He, too, sat down behind a blanket his mother had hung in front of his sleeping mat as a kind of makeshift bedroom wall. Pressing his face to the soft material, he pictured the man's smile beyond its thread and listened.

"Amir," the man said, gesturing to himself and still smiling.

Zayd's father nodded and cleared his throat to speak.

"Moosa."

Amir then began to tell Moosa of a school—a school Amir oversaw—that many children in the camp attended. It had all started from a dream, Amir said, a dream of a school that welcomed refugee children.

Zayd sat up from his hiding place. Before he gave it any thought, he peeked his head around the corner of the blanket. If Amir saw him, he did not let on, though Zayd suspected he did; his voice grew lighter, warmer, as he spoke to Zayd's baba.

"We teach all the subjects the children need to learn: math, writing, geography, English, science, even art. We teach them also about Jesus. We are a Christian school, so we share with the children about God, about our Savior, Jesus Christ."

Amir stopped, smiling at Moosa, as if nothing shameful had left his mouth. Moosa nodded again, rubbing his beard in contemplation. Now leaning so far beyond the blanket that his head and torso revealed themselves, Zayd risked falling over. But his curiosity overtook him. He leaned further, his elbow wobbling beneath him, and dropped to the floor of the tent with a soft thud. Before either his father or Amir could see him, Zayd crawled back onto his mat behind the blanket. His mind crowded with thoughts about their conversation.

The smiling man came to talk about me going to school. Years have passed since I have gone to a school! For so long, I have only known this place: rows and rows of tents, each one just like the next, the constant noise of too many people in too small a space, the smells that make my nose crinkle. Baba and Mama tried, but the schools in the city won't let me in. Why does this school of infidels want me?

Outside the confines of his mind, Zayd realized that Amir and his baba had finished speaking. Amir had stood, and his baba responded saying that he would think about it. Amir seemed to expect this response and nodded in agreement. Then, for the first time, he turned toward Zayd, still smiling, and said, "Zayd, I hope we will see you in class very soon." Then, he walked out of the tent into the white, hot sunlight.

A DECISION MADE

Amir returned a handful of times after his first visit. Each time he came, he shared something different about the school: its students, its teachers, its lessons. As a fuller picture of it unfolded in Zayd's mind, his anticipation grew. But in all those weeks, Zayd's baba did not share his thoughts about the school with his son.

Zayd heard his father pray to Allah each night that Amir came, asking for guidance. One day, he saw the excitement in his father's movements when he heard from his neighbors that Amir had come to the camp again; they had glimpsed him making his way through the tents. Displaying their small store of food in between their only two chairs, Moosa awaited his guest, a new question ready on his lips. He had rehearsed his questions a few times aloud, unknowingly within Zayd's hearing.

Amir entered wearing his signature smile, greeted Moosa, and nodded to Zayd, not-so-hidden in his usual corner. He took a seat in one of the small chairs. Moosa solemnly offered him a paper cup filled with dates, then the two men began the longest conversation they had entered into yet.

When Amir left nearly two hours later, Zayd's father called for his wife.

"Let us discuss the matter outside," Moosa whispered to her as she tightened her hijab around her head, winked at her son, and followed.

Zayd's breath slowed, his heartbeat pounding in his ears, as he waited for his parents' response. The tangerine light of the afternoon filtering through their tent had abated with the arrival of the moon. When his baba stepped back into their tent, Moosa's eyes immediately found his son. Zayd could not recall a time he had ever remained so still.

"We will allow you to attend the school."

The entire world opened up before Zayd as he imagined the classes, the teachers, the other students his age. His face wore a smile like Amir's, and he laughed aloud, sweeping his mother into a hug so tight that she laughed.

I never thought that I would go to a school where these Christians teach. But I do not care about their false religion. Amir has shown how much I can learn from them, all the questions they can answer for me! I cannot wait to go to school again!

A DREAM DIVERTED

A few days later, Zayd found himself huddled once more in the corner of the family tent, waiting. Uncertainty had replaced the joy and possibility he had felt at his parent's initial decision to send him to school. He could taste the tang of his own fear on his tongue and tried to swallow it down. As a man, his baba told him, Zayd could not walk in fear.

He recalled the conversation his father had with a stranger just hours before—a conversation that changed the course of his life, just as he had believed the one with Amir would. The day before Zayd's first day of classes at Amir's school, a crooked-eyed man walked into their family's tent. Though short and dressed plainly, the man had filled the room with boundless anger coming off of him in waves. He felt—Zayd struggled to find the word—*wrong*, so very different from Amir.

Zayd looked at his father, a question in his eyes. *This man, what did he want?* But his baba did not return his glance, a mixture of weariness and pain on his face. Zayd only caught three words of his father's conversation with this man: job, pay, and the name of their old country. He would soon learn the man had come to their tent with a promise of work for Zayd and a steady paycheck to send back to Zayd's family. As soon as his father told him of the offer, Zayd knew his baba could not refuse it. And he didn't.

Zayd would not attend school. He would leave, back to the place from which they fled so many years before.

His mother's tears began to fall then. Zayd wanted to reach out to her, hold her in his arms and tell her he would make her proud, but he only turned toward his corner of the tent, stepped behind the blanket, and began to roll up his mat. Baba had told him he needed to exhibit strength, act as a man should, despite the overwhelming fear and dread coursing through him. His mother's cries grew louder, filling the tent. The warmth of the sun through its canvas felt stifling now, like the thought of the faraway desert soon to greet him.

A DIFFERENT FUTURE

Weeks had come and gone since the crooked-eyed man entered their tent. As he sat now in a cluster of men listening to orders from their superiors, Zayd shuddered inside. At least his family did not know the truth: that his father had unknowingly agreed to enlist him in a radical group filled with known fanatics and murderers. Zayd looked down at the weapon in his hands. He could not count the number of questions he feared he would never have answered.

The cold faces of the men around him, like their weapons, struck him with anguish. Zayd tried to remember Amir's smiling face and the hope that he had filled his family's tent with, a blessed hope, the hope of a different future. Gripping his weapon tighter, Zayd tried to believe that one day, that same hope would find him again.

LIGHT IN THE DARKNESS

According to a 2022 report released by the United Nations, Syria had the second highest rate of recruitment and use of children as soldiers in 2021, with 1,301 children suffering this fate.[5] Families in refugee camps are particularly vulnerable as these radical groups exploit their circumstances to indoctrinate new members. *How is God working in the midst of this challenge?* Christian schools offer hope of a new pathway where children can step out of their circumstance, receive an education, and learn about Jesus. Zayd's story is real and deeply saddened the Ananias House team. We praise the Lord, however, that he encountered teachers like Amir before he left. We have no way of knowing how the seeds Amir planted may bear fruit in Zayd's life, but we see throughout Scripture that God uses difficult circumstances to draw people to Himself and bring glory to His name.

I planted, Apollos watered, but God was causing the growth. So then neither the one who plants nor the one who waters is anything, but God who causes the growth. - **1 Corinthians 3:6-7 (NASB)**

6

NADIA
زارية

Nadia awoke to the sound of erratic breathing. She reached out her hand to touch her sister, needing to feel something, someone, *real*. She felt Farah flinch at her touch, then clasp her hand and squeeze it.

Their mother's muffled cries echoed from across the room. Nadia peered into the shadows, her eyes finally adjusting to the dark until she made out the form of her mother to their far right and her little brother, Malik, a small outline at their far left. While her mother nearly doubled over at the intensity of her sobbing, Nadia's seven-year-old brother sat stiffly against the wall. With his head fixed directly forward, Malik seemed entranced, just as he had when their captors entered the room and forced him to watch the assault of his mother and sisters. Nadia felt droplets on her chin and quickly swiped her fingers across her face, almost surprised to find her cheeks stained with tears.

Will rescue ever come?

The events of the last few hours encircled her consciousness, but she would not—could not—let them in. She had to stay focused, stay alert. She clenched her sister's hand to keep the memories at bay, only loosening her grip when she heard Farah's painful intake of breath.

At that moment, the door to their dark prison swung open, a light from the hall flooding in.

RANSOMED

Nadia could not recall the last time she saw the moon in full view, or felt a nighttime breeze run its fingers through her long hair. But there they stood, on an empty street beneath a navy expanse of sky, all four of them alive, as their father herded them gently into his waiting car. He had secured his family's release.

Weeks had passed since the radicals took them, Nadia learned. Weeks before her father, Abdul, could secure the funds to buy back the freedom of his wife and three children. Now, gathered together in his small car, Nadia studied her father's face as they drove west. She could still see the faint bruises on his face, the missing teeth, his mangled hands.

So, they had hurt him, too.

She clung to Farah's hand—she had not let go since they left that house—and stole a glance at her little brother. He remained in a trance, sitting pinned against the car seat, gazing lifelessly out of the windshield. Their mother did the same.

They had their freedom now. A new country rose before them beyond the hills. But despite this, Nadia still felt trapped within the dark of that terrible room. As she looked at her family, she wondered if they felt trapped, too.

GREETED

After arriving in their new country, the family fell into a rhythm of normalcy which enabled them to function as other refugees did. They moved into a one-bedroom apartment, which they shared with another family, and tried to make the best of every day. But despite this new beginning, joy eluded them. Nadia and Farah did not play with the neighborhood's children, rarely leaving home. Malik helped his father, following him around town to do odd jobs, but he did not speak. Nadia could not recall the last time she had heard her brother's voice.

But as winter drew near and the odd jobs Abdul worked grew fewer and fewer, Nadia's family began to feel the pangs of malnutrition. This did not shock Nadia—she had seen the refugee camps, the rows and rows of underfed families—but she had hoped God would mercifully provide for theirs, having seen what they went through.

Nadia knew that her family believed in Jesus, but they rarely attended church services together, and she had little understanding of what it meant to identify as "Christian." She had a vague knowledge of bad feelings between Christians and Muslims throughout their home country, but this did not seem to affect her family, who did not go out of their way to associate with either group. Rather, they kept to themselves. But even that did not prevent the kidnapping or the nightmare they endured.

One day, while playing with Farah outside their apartment, Nadia overheard a group of boys talking about a place, a church, where people gave out food. The boys began to walk purposefully, some breaking out into a jog, down the right side of the street. Nadia tugged on her sister's sleeve and motioned for them to follow.

The girls trailed the boys at a short distance. As they rounded a few corners, she saw a church with a cross hung prominently in front of the building. While the group of boys ran up the steps together, undaunted by their quest, Nadia and Farah halted across the street.

Food. Finally.

"Let's go tell Mama," Nadia whispered to her sister.

An hour later, the girls returned to the church with their mother in tow. Her daughters clinging to the back of her skirt, Sara walked with determination into the building. A smiling woman greeted the trio and held out her hand to them.

"Welcome sister, we are so happy to see you," the woman said.

She clasped Sara's hands in both of her own.

"How can we help you?"

Her mother stared at the woman, unspeaking. She seemed startled by the woman's touch, by her smile, by her eyes, so full of neighborly concern.

Nadia barely heard her mother's response, said in a whisper: "We are hungry."

The woman nodded, leading Sara to a corner of the large chapel where a man behind a fold-out table sat with a stack of food vouchers. He handed them several, his smile as genuine as the woman's.

"Please come back when you need more," she said.

As Sara, Nadia, and Farah turned to leave, the woman spoke again.

"We have a service on Sundays. We would love to see you there. You are always welcome."

Sara thanked the woman, took Nadia and Farah by the hand, and exited the building. On their walk home, Nadia watched as tears fell silently from her mother's face.

REDEEMED

Nadia and her family continued to receive vouchers over the next several weeks and even attended church services on Sundays. Hearing the pastor preach from the Bible, listening to the words of the hymns that called her "beloved," stirred something warm inside of Nadia.

One song they sang had the word "redemption," which puzzled her. She did not understand it and later asked Mary—the woman who had first greeted them at the church, now her mother's closest and only friend— what "redemption" meant.

"It is something wonderful that Jesus made possible on the cross," Mary said. "You see, people who are dead in sin and evil, He makes alive in Him, new creations."

But can He redeem me?

For weeks, Nadia wondered about this "redemption." Could God really redeem her from the shame of her family's captivity? From what happened to her, her sister, her mother and her brother in the dark of that house at the hands of their captors? Could He really heal them?

As she sang out this hymn about God's redemption, Nadia felt that same warmth within her spreading. With every note, she felt lighter, weightless even—*free*. For the first time in her life, she felt God's presence and believed that He truly loved her.

This belief only grew over the next several months, during which time Nadia and her family's lives slowly began to change. She and her siblings started attending school at their new church, and from the Christian teachers there, learned more about Jesus than they ever had before.

Nadia found herself quicker to laugh and smile with the other children at school. She even dreamed about her future, thoughts that she had not entertained since before the kidnapping. She and Farah joined their church's worship team, singing every Sunday before the whole congregation, Nadia's favorite time of the week. Malik, who had not spoken in months, finally began to talk to other children, and, word by word, to his family at dinnertime. He, too, eventually joined his sisters on the worship team.

The school's handful of teachers had gradually become mentors to the three siblings. In between their courses, they prayed with them, and over time, began to understand without a word from Nadia or her siblings that the family had undergone terrible trauma. Over tea, two teachers tactfully inquired of Nadia's parents what their lives looked like in their old country. After that conversation, they poured their love upon the children with abandon. As a result, the children grew more and more open.

Nadia and Farah spoke quietly to each other in bed before sleep every night, talking about their school, their teachers, their church, and Jesus. They agreed that they had never known what God's love felt like before they entered the church that day for food vouchers alongside their mother.

RETURNED

Several years later, just as Nadia turned 18, war broke out. Her father decided that he had to get his family to safety, and soon, an opportunity arose for them to escape to America. But Nadia did not want to leave.

A few years before, she had met a passionate, caring boy at church and they had fallen in love. He felt called, he said, to pastor a church, and, together, they dreamed of the church they would one day plant.

But Nadia understood her father wanted to protect his family, that they had endured so much at the hands of their captors, and he did not want them to experience pain like that again. So, with her family, Nadia left their church, their home, their community, and her love, to escape the war.

Yet, Nadia's sojourn in America did not last long. As soon as they arrived, she made plans in her heart to return.

"Why would you want to return to a place of such trauma, where war breaks out everywhere?" one of her new American friends asked her once she and her family had settled.

Nadia paused for a long time, trying to find the words.

How can I stay away from the place where I first encountered my God?

Nadia knew that once she returned to the region from which her family fled, she could not come back to the U.S. and might never see her family again. She considered the gravity of her decision, the long-term implications it would have on her life. She also thought about her experiences in her home country and the pervasive darkness she had endured as a child. Finally, she pictured in her mind the many families still in that darkness, still unaware of the redeeming love of God.

I will return.

LIGHT IN THE DARKNESS

According to a 2022 Global Peace Index, the MENA region is the least peaceful region in the world and has held that spot for 7 consecutive years.⁶ Radical groups still exert dominance in various areas, consistently leaving trauma and fear in their wake. As a result, MENA children have witnessed and endured horrific things. *How is God working in the midst of this challenge?* The church alone voices the hope of Jesus Christ, and through these Christian communities, God enables the healing of deep trauma. Ananias House team members witnessed the transformation of Nadia, Farah, and Malik after just one year in Christian community. Years afterward, Nadia left the haven of America to return to a war-torn country and marry the young man she had fallen in love with at church. God raised him up as a pastor, and, together, they went on to plant a church in the city where they met. In the years since then, God has used them to bring many people to Himself.

Do not be overcome by evil, but overcome evil with good. - **Romans 12:21**

7

HASSAN

حسن

"Next week, students, we will discuss why Jesus Christ came to earth."

As his teacher wrapped up the day's lesson, Hassan's mind wandered to what awaited him at home. He knew that his father would be gone again, searching for work that seemed impossible to find. His mother, however, would greet him at the door, a smile fixed on her face. Though tired all the time, that smile never left her. Hassan did not know why; throughout the day, she searched their kitchen cupboards over and over as if food might suddenly appear. It never did.

Every day, the family experienced hunger, especially Hassan, who had grown three inches in only a few months. As Hassan's father knew too well, jobs numbered fewer and fewer. The value of their country's currency diminished daily, too, requiring more money to buy fewer quantities of food. Even the most basic things—rice, milk, toilet paper, bandages—had become difficult to find.

With six siblings, Hassan intuited his parent's desperation, but he could also see it in the looks they often exchanged. He had even overheard them discussing the possibility of arranging a marriage for his 15-year-old sister, Laila. A good marriage would provide for her and offer additional resources to the family, they had mused. Hassan knew that if his sister heard their idea, it would terrify her.

But as their hunger grew between the meals they could scrounge, so did the family's shame. Hassan felt this shame more acutely than any of his siblings. At 14, he considered himself a leader in the home. His duty rested in helping his father provide so that their family's hunger and resulting shame would not dishonor them any further. Believing this wholeheartedly, Hassan had tried to find work like his father, asking his classmates at school if they knew of any jobs in the area for kids their age. The other children met him with blank stares so that he often came home disappointed.

"Your job is school, habibi," his mother would say.

Hassan's education at the local Christian school would, his parents reminded him, provide him with far greater opportunities than any local job. But years would pass before he finished school, and he could not wait years to help his parents. Besides, Hassan did not enjoy school lately. While he loved math and science and found his teachers' lessons about the Christian God fascinating—even inspiring—he fumbled over English words that his friends had mastered months before, which made all the girls in his class giggle. Hassan hated this; he found it hard enough to speak to girls in Arabic.

When the final bell rang through the halls of the school, Hassan could not wait to get out of class and meet his best friend, Nadeem, for the walk home. He had spent most of the day drawing airplanes and their corresponding engines in the back pages of his English notebook. If only he knew how to fly planes, he could take him and Nadeem and their families far, far away.

Hassan greeted Nadeem with a fist bump, and they began to walk home, a comfortable silence settling between them. He heard Nadeem's stomach growl but did not acknowledge it so as not to embarrass his friend. Nadeem's family struggled to find food, too.

As they rounded the first street corner that led them into their neighborhood, a man approached them. He wore new clothes. So new, Hassan noted, that the man looked very out of place. As he drew closer, Hassan and Nadeem both stopped, fear and uncertainty immobilizing them. The man had a strangely confident gait, almost a strut, and when he opened his mouth, Hassan felt himself flinch.

"How would you like to earn some money?" he asked the boys.

Why us? Is our hunger so obvious?

Hassan did not voice these questions; he worried that his parents would consider speaking to this man a shameful act. And yet, his family continued to starve day after day. They continued to discuss marrying his sister to a stranger from another country.

Hassan and Nadeem glanced at one another, wary but curious.

"What kind of job?" Hassan finally asked.

The man did not share many details, only that the job might take a few days to complete, but the money satisfied any reservations they might have. Hassan did not trust the man—something dwelt in his wide, green eyes that filled Hassan with a deep foreboding. And yet this opportunity could help Hassan and Nadeem feed their families. It could even, Hassan prayed, stop his parents from having Laila marry.

When first Hassan and then Nadeem nodded their heads, the man gave them a time and location to meet his associate on the following day.

"They will give you instructions when you get there," he said gruffly.

They?

Hassan and Nadeem risked another glance at each other before the man turned and walked away.

THE INVISIBLE BOYS

The next morning, Hassan and Nadeem met at the back of their school. They had devised a plan on their walk home the day before to skip their classes. Stashing their backpacks behind the building's metal waste bin, they straightened their shoulders and strolled calmly to the location the man had given them, a 20-minute walk from their neighborhood. They traveled silently, a feeling of uncertainty hanging between them.

Have we made a mistake accepting this man's offer?

Adrenaline high, hearts racing, the boys followed the address to a vacant convenience store parking lot. Several men stood at the back of the building, the waistband of their jeans bulging where Hassan and Nadeem knew they hid guns.

As the two boys approached the group of men, all eyes rested on one in particular—their leader. Turning toward Hassan first, this man gave him a small piece of shredded paper filled with tiny, Arabic scrawl and, with a slight accent, instructed Hassan to hide it in his shoe. Then, he gave Hassan another address to memorize, along with a code word.

"The man who answers and asks for the code word—make sure he gets it. No one else."

Another of the men handed Nadeem a small, wrapped package, pulling him aside to give him special instructions of his own. Shaking, Nadeem did not reply.

When the men finished giving their instructions, they turned their backs on Hassan and Nadeem and resumed their conversation, a cold dismissal of the new errand boys. Hassan shot Nadeem a parting look of unconvincing assurance. They hesitated for just a moment, glanced back at the men, and then took off running in opposite directions.

The longer that he ran, the more fearful Hassan grew. This area of the city had a dangerous reputation; his father and uncles had warned him against it. But as he walked, he realized that nobody looked in his direction. Nobody seemed to care about this small boy weaving through crowds and cars. As Hassan continued toward the address, he felt completely invisible.

Suddenly it dawned on him why the man had approached him and Nadeem. He needed his couriers to be invisible, and few people would think twice about seeing a starving boy running through back alleys. Nobody knew them or cared.

Hassan kept his head down, trying to walk confidently. The address he had memorized led him to a battered house on the corner of a dirt road, the windows busted in by what seemed like thrown bricks. He knocked tentatively on the door. It swung open while his fist hung in the air.

The man who greeted him had thick glasses and thinning hair. He held his hand out to Hassan expectantly. Hassan stared at him a moment, then quickly retrieved the folded paper from his shoe. The man huffed at Hassan, read it, then yanked him by his shirt so that Hassan's face floated an inch from his own. He smelled sour.

"Tell no one, or there will be more of this," he said.

He slapped Hassan hard across the face. Hassan stumbled back as the door slammed and locked. So, he would courier messages between these cruel, mysterious men.

As Hassan arrived back at the original meeting place, the man in charge looked him over, a smirk on his face.

"It looks like things went well. You're alive, at least."

Nadeem stood in the shadows by the fence as if in fear of another errand. He, too, looked as if he had received a beating. Bruises darkened across his face, and from the way he held his stomach, Hassan suspected he had taken a beating in other places, too.

"I've got another client who could use your services if you're interested," the man said, handing each of the boys their wages.

The well-dressed stranger had not lied—the money, though not much, amounted to the most Hassan and Nadeem had seen in weeks.

If I could do more jobs like this, then perhaps Baba would not have to force Laila to marry. And we could buy food today. Maybe soon, a new heater! No more shivering at night.

WHERE THE MONEY LEADS

The well-dressed man had connections all over the city, even into the countryside. He also worked with people on both sides of their country's conflict, which did not appear to bother him.

"Wherever the money leads," he would say.

Some jobs took a few hours, others took days and left the boys bleary-eyed and, more often than not, beaten. They never asked questions, fearing that if they said too much or lingered too long at a location, they would return home with fewer teeth. If they thought of escaping their situation, Hassan and Nadeem did not share that with each other. Their "manager," or so they called him with derision, always seemed nearby, lurking around the boys' school and even, they dreaded to discover, their homes.

Hassan's parents did not question, despite the concern on their faces, where the money came from. His mother asked once, but when Hassan would not reply, she did not press him any further. Their desperation drove them to a resigned silence. At Hassan's suggestion—he had truly become a new leader in the family—his baba bought a heater, and the family crowded around it at night to listen to the uncles tell stories of the old, better days of their youth.

But at school, Hassan's teachers noticed his absences. They began to regularly pull him aside on the days he did attend. They did the same with Nadeem. The boys' mutual silences seemed to trouble the teachers, who Hassan knew cared more about their students than most from the way they always tried to teach them about God in addition to their school subjects.

One day, Ms. Miriam, the English teacher, brought Hassan into her classroom, where another teacher, Mr. Aaban, sat waiting.

As Hassan entered, Mr. Aaban offered him a seat next to him.

"Are you okay, Hassan? Ms. Miriam and I worry about you. Both you and Nadeem have missed a lot of school. We can help you catch up on your assignments. But we really want to help you with whatever has caused your absences lately."

The worry in Mr. Aaban's eyes unsettled Hassan, and he could feel the tears sting his own. But he shook his head.

Stop asking me. Stop asking me. Stop asking.

Hassan tried desperately to find the right words if only to make his teachers stop inquiring about his absences, stop trying to help him. But despite himself, he contemplated their offer. He had gotten very behind in math and science, his favorite subjects. He wanted to learn what he had missed. Hassan placed his hands over his face and thought deeply, frantically, about what to say.

Maybe I should just drop out. I cannot keep my new job and go to school. But I feel free here, free from the well-dressed man, free from more and more beatings. Here, I feel peace.

When Hassan pulled his hands away from his face, Ms. Miriam and Mr. Aaban continued to study him with patient concern.

"This peace in the school comes from God. Not Allah, but Jesus."

Hassan had heard Ms. Miriam say this once. His eyes roved his teachers' faces in return.

It must be because of Jesus that our teachers love us enough to notice Nadeem and I were gone so many times. "We love because He first loved us," Ms. Miriam had said. Well, Jesus, I am praying to you now. I want your peace. I want to stay in school.

After a shaky breath, the story came pouring out of Hassan, like a floodgate had burst open in his soul. When he finished, Mr. Aaban, with tears in his eyes, told Hassan not to risk his life in this way, that his life had too great a value in God's eyes.

"Besides," Mr. Aaban pleaded. "This man you speak of—his requests have no end. He does not mind if what he asks kills you and Nadeem. He can find others. But your family, including your teachers and friends here at school, only have one Hassan. One Nadeem. Both made in God's image."

Surprised at the relief he felt, Hassan wept in Mr. Aaban and Ms. Miriam's arms. For the first time since they completed their initial errand, Hassan believed it possible for he and Nadeem to escape. To escape the well-dressed man. To escape hunger. To escape death at the hands of both. Maybe not today, maybe not in the way he hoped. But even the smallest hope of a better tomorrow felt worthy to believe in.

As the final school bell rang, Mr. Aaban and Ms. Miriam placed their hands over Hassan's head in unison and prayed in the name of Jesus.

LIGHT IN THE DARKNESS

According to a report published by the United Nations in 2022, the standard cost of food necessary for survival increased in Lebanon by 1,484% since October 2019, with 69% of families reducing the number of meals they ate daily to compensate.* These desperate circumstances increase the risk of violence, human trafficking, sexual exploitation, drug addiction, and indoctrination into radical thinking. Hassan found himself entangled in a dark world but saw no way out. *How is God working in the midst of this challenge?* Hassan's Christian school gave him the opportunity to learn about Jesus and to engage with people who modeled fellowship, prayer, and worship. The teachers discipled him, offering Hassan the protection he so desired and the hope of true freedom.

"But if you can do anything, have compassion on us and help us." And Jesus said to him, "If you can? All things are possible for one who believes." Immediately the father of the child cried out and said, "I believe; help my unbelief!" - **Mark 9:22b - 24**

ZARIA
زارية

"How was school today?" asked Zaria's mother when she pushed open the door to their apartment, hurried into the kitchen, set her backpack down, and dug into the awaiting snack: labneh with olive oil and za'atar.

"Fine," Zaria lied, mouth full of savory spices.

She did not want to tell her mother about the awful names the girls at school called her or how she had done poorly on a quiz. She wanted to save those confessions for her most trusted friend.

The moment Zaria finished her snack, she ran out of the apartment to visit Ms. Lili.

Ms. Lili, a kind, older widow, had lived next door to Zaria and her family for years. Zaria spent every free moment she could with Ms. Lili, not only because she loved her, but because her apartment seemed the dwelling place of love itself. Everywhere she glanced perched a different kind of plant which Ms. Lili somehow managed to keep alive. Along the brightly colored walls hung many framed photos of Ms. Lili's family and her travels around the world with her husband. Zaria did not know Ms. Lili's age, but the lines on her face told a story of many experiences, many smiles. Zaria felt safe with her, safer and happier than with anyone else.

Zaria heard her mother's voice calling after her to knock on Ms. Lili's door, not to just barge in. But Ms. Lili usually left her door slightly ajar around the hour Zaria and her little brother, Adam, returned from school.

She knocked on the open door anyway, and Ms. Lili soon appeared, smiling as usual. Her graying hair sat piled atop her head, errant curls falling happily around her face.

After finishing a pot of fresh tea and a whole plate of baklava, which Ms. Lili made herself, the two sat together on cushions in the living room and opened the large blue Bible that Ms. Lili carried with her everywhere.

Together, they read a few chapters. Zaria loved hearing the stories in the Bible. She loved the lilt of Ms. Lili's voice as she read aloud and the way her face shone with joy as she explained to Zaria the promises of God. Ms. Lili treasured every word in her Bible, which made Zaria treasure them, too.

On an afternoon in which dusk came sooner than Zaria desired, they closed the great blue Bible, bookmarking their place in the book of Esther, and said goodbye. Ms. Lili hugged Zaria tightly and handed her a pack of leftover baklava to share with her parents and brother.

"Remember, Zaria," Ms. Lili said. "Even when we don't feel God with us, He is there. He never leaves us."

Zaria nodded and wrapped her arms around Ms. Lili for a final hug goodbye. She couldn't wait to see her again.

THE SILENT GUEST

As Zaria walked unwillingly toward her own apartment, she looked up, startled, to find the door cracked open. Pushing inside, she saw several unfamiliar suitcases in the entryway, their surfaces scratched, their wheels caked with mud.

Slipping her shoes off, Zaria tiptoed noiselessly toward the dining room where voices emanated from within.

It took a moment for her parents to notice her presence amid the chaotic scene before them. When they did, they ushered her closer.

"Zaria, there you are! Don't just stand there gaping," her father scolded. "Help us welcome our family from the north. They will stay with us until they are able to move into their own home."

The strange faces before her nodded and waved as her father introduced an uncle, an aunt, and several cousins. Their names quickly slipped out of Zaria's mind at the sight of the tallest man in the room, whom her father had introduced as "Uncle Khalil." He had a full beard and eyebrows that met in the middle. He reminded Zaria of a wolf, or a bear. She felt like small prey under his gaze, which lingered on her and intensified in what Zaria felt to be a very long moment. When her father turned back to visit with the group again, she scurried away to find her brother.

BIRDSONG

Zaria hoped that her cousins would play with her and Adam or tell stories after dinner about where they'd come from. To her disappointment, they largely ignored her, only conversing with her father when he spoke to them first. Zaria could tell that they only responded to him out of politeness. Each of them seemed trapped in their own thoughts as they jockeyed for space in the too-crowded apartment; six new additions to the family of four had left little space for individual privacy.

No one spoke of what prompted them to move. In fact, Zaria only heard her parents speak of the new guests in whispers: *"Have they told you of their plans? How long must we host them?"*

Uncle Khalil, as the head of his large family, might have tried to repay Zaria's father for his hospitality by helping him fix whatever broke in the apartment—the heater and toilet seemed to break often now with excessive use—but he did not contribute to the household, and he spoke least of all of them. Zaria observed that he spent his days staring for hours at a time out of their living room window, a view which offered little apart from the sun peaking over the jewelry shop across the street.

His gaze continued to linger on Zaria, too. As she walked through the apartment, she felt his wolf eyes stalking her as if readying for a hunt.

Her mother caught Uncle Khalil watching Zaria only once. Afterward, she hurried into the kitchen to speak to her husband, where Zaria heard her not-so-quietly whisper, *"Shouldn't he at least be looking for a job?"*

Uncle Khalil did not join them for dinner but ate his meals in the guest room, where he slept odd hours. Zaria heard him pacing in the middle of the night, even stepping out into the hall at times. While this made her uneasy, Adam's curiosity about their uncle produced in Zaria a wary interest, too: he had scars all over his arms, as if he had jumped through glass at some point and landed on its shards. And he could make strange, whistling sounds with his mouth, which captivated Adam most of all.

"Like living with many different birds," Adam had murmured one night after hearing Uncle Khalil in his room.

But these noises—the only delightful thing about Uncle Khalil that Zaria could find—soon signified danger and made her tremble with fear.

One night as Zaria lay in her bed thinking over her day, a verse began repeating itself in her mind. Ms. Lili had taught it to her: *"Trust in the Lord with all your heart, and do not lean on your understanding. In all your ways acknowledge him, and he will make straight your paths."* As Zaria reflected on this, she suddenly heard birdsong just outside her and Adam's bedroom door. Her pulse quickened.

Uncle Khalil.

The tweeting grew louder, then mingled with the squeak of a turning doorknob, then, after a pause, with the soft thud of the door closing again.

Zaria could not move. A terror greater than any fear she had ever known held her body so still that even her breath slowed. Just as she began to fear for her little brother, she felt the distinct downward pull of a heavy body seating itself beside her on the bed.

IN THE NAME OF THE LORD JESUS

The next morning, Zaria finished her breakfast in silence. Instead of waiting for her brother as she usually did during their remaining minutes before the walk to school, she hurried out into the hall toward Ms. Lili's closed door. Forming a fist to knock, she hesitated with her hand in the air.

Would Ms. Lili still want to be my friend now? Would anyone?

Tears threatened to fall. But despite feeling ashamed and confused, Zaria knew she needed to find somewhere safe. For her, *safe* meant Ms. Lili's home. *Safe* meant Ms. Lili herself.

So, she knocked gently against the door, her knuckles barely gracing the wood. Worried Ms. Lili didn't hear her, Zaria started to knock again when, gratefully, the door swung open.

Ms. Lili looked down in surprise to see Zaria in her school clothes. Zaria never came to see her before school.

"Come in," she invited with a warm, puzzled smile.

After offering Zaria tea and fresh pita, which Zaria surprisingly heard herself decline, Ms. Lili came to sit beside her in the living room, where just the day before they had finished reading the book of Proverbs.

"Has something happened, Zaria?"

Pressing her trembling lips together, Zaria did not speak. When Ms. Lili reached for her hand, Zaria snatched it out of reach and burrowed both of her hands in her pockets. She felt so out of place now in Ms. Lili's home, as if she no longer belonged there—as if she stained its goodness with her shameful presence.

Ms. Lili watched her carefully, a question forming in her eyes. But as she continued to observe Zaria, the question soon became something like anger, then, something closer to rage. Zaria had never seen this look on Ms. Lili's face before.

All of a sudden, Ms. Lili rose, opened her door again, walked across the hall, and knocked. Zaria could then hear her mother's voice. As the two women spoke, her mother's tone changed from one of surprise to concern.

"Something has happened to Zaria," she heard Ms. Lili say. "And I suspect I know what. Please, come to my apartment, you and your husband and Adam for dinner tonight. The children can play in the next room while we adults speak."

"Your guests must stay behind," Ms. Lili added forcefully.

A long silence followed Ms. Lili's request. Zaria found herself crumpling her shirt in her fists, anger filling her small frame until it shook. She hated her uncle. And if her mother did not accept Ms. Lili's invitation, she would hate her, too.

Then, in her mind, a gentle voice spoke, countering these thoughts.

Trust in the Lord...He is always with us.

"Please," Zaria heard Ms. Lili say again, this time in a softer, urgent tone.

"In the name of the Lord Jesus, please come, and bring the children with you as soon as they are home from school."

"Okay," Zaria heard her mother reply. "We will come."

LIGHT IN THE DARKNESS

According to a 2021 UN report, UNICEF and their partners handled 5,621 cases of child abuse and exploitation in Lebanon between October 2020-2021, a 44% increase over the previous year.[3] Though this number is staggering, many cases of sexual abuse go unreported, so the real total of cases of abuse and exploitation is likely much higher. As homes become uncomfortably crowded due to the region's conflict and financial collapse, the likelihood of boys and girls suffering abuse increases, and prosecution rarely occurs. *How is God working in the midst of this challenge?* Zaria suffered abuse at the hands of a previously unknown relative, and due to the honor-shame culture around her, felt she could not voice it without consequence. Yet, she encountered Christ through the kindness of her neighbor, Ms. Lili, who discipled and equipped Zaria with Scripture. Thankfully, Ms. Lili recognized the signs of abuse and courageously sought to bring it to light.

So she called the name of the LORD who spoke to her, "You are a God of seeing," for she said, "Truly here I have seen him who looks after me." - **Genesis 16:13**

NYLAH

نايلة

"Are you composing in your head again?"

Lina entered her and her sister's pink-themed bedroom, teeth freshly brushed and giving off a minty aroma.

"You have that dreamy look you get when the notes come together."

Nylah considered this and smiled as she changed into her nightclothes.

"I was actually thinking about how Baba's singing reminds me more of a toad's than a man's."

The girls tumbled onto their beds in fits of giggles, full and happy. Their mother had prepared their favorite dinner that evening—shish kabobs, with baklava for dessert—and their father had attempted his hand at the piano, playing rather poorly and singing even worse. When Nylah caught her breath, her stomach releasing the taut pressure of too much laughter, she rolled onto her side and took up the stack of colorful drawings on her bedside table.

Her mother had hosted tea for some of their female neighbors the day before, while Nylah entertained their children with songs on the piano, stories, and crafts. Her smile deepened at the memory, her fingers tracing the children's names across the tops of the pages. She had helped each child sign their artwork and promised to display it proudly on the wall above her bed. Their delighted squeals still rang through her mind.

"They adore you," Lina encouraged her younger sister, leisurely passing her a roll of tape as she spoke.

"Not just the children in our building, either. You seem to know every child in the neighborhood. It amazes me how you can remember so many of their names."

Nylah shrugged as she rose and began taping the drawings to her wall.

"I don't know all of them."

Nylah knew Lina meant the children of the Christians. Their parents forbade Lina and Nylah from interacting with them, with anyone who worshiped the prophet Jesus as God. Worried about their exposure to infidel teaching, their mother guarded the girls against even speaking to their Christian neighbors. The family name held too much honor, too much sway, among their community to risk tarnishing with unwise friendships, she told them. Nylah did not understand, and it saddened her.

"The birds keep acting so strangely tonight. I hope they stop so we can get some sleep," Lina murmured, changing the subject as she nestled under her covers.

Outside their window sounded the flutter and song of a multitude of pigeons flocking together in the sky.

Nylah gazed out of their fourth-story window, nodding her head in agreement. She shivered, thankful for the warmth of her hand-knit blankets on such a cold night. Turning off the crystal lamp on the nightstand, she crawled into bed, listening for the telltale slowing of her sister's breath as she fell into a deep sleep. What a good day—what a good week! She did not know a family more blessed than theirs and anticipated the new joys tomorrow might bring.

"Good night, Lina," she whispered happily.

"Sleep well."

SHAKEN GROUND

The cold reached her first, penetrating through her shock. Nylah blinked against the dust that now filled the air and made her eyes burn. The awful, deafening sound of rock grinding against rock still echoed in her ears. Why could she not see? Why did it smell like fire? Why did she feel so thirsty? Why did her throat feel coated with smoke—hadn't she just spoken, just told Lina goodnight?

Lina.

Before she could call out for her sister, Nylah felt desperate hands grasp her chest and shoulders. They yanked her up and out of bed by her arms. Panic propelled Nylah forward to follow her mother, who urgently dragged her out of the room and into the hall, where her father and Lina stood waiting for them.

The family descended the stairs two by two until they emerged onto the street. Behind their parents, the girls whimpered in fear and pain at how tightly each parent clutched them by the hand, Nylah by her mother and Lina by her father.

As they drew closer to the entryway of their building, despairing wails began to mingle with shrieks of pain, a symphony of sorrow that struck Nylah as the most horrible sound she had ever heard. When they reached the landing of their building, they joined in a small crowd of neighbors all rushing to the street, too, their faces masks of shock and disbelief.

Shoeless and clothed in pajamas, Nylah and her family sprinted together across the street just in time to turn and watch their apartment building— and several more down the street—collapse into a heap of rubble.

A piercing cry sounded from Nylah's lips. All of her things, all of her memories...buried.

"Where can we go?"

Nylah's mother clung to her baba's elbow.

"What do we do?"

Her baba did not respond.

A female neighbor stood a few feet away, motionless and staring at where their building used to stand. Nylah recalled she had two little daughters. The three of them had attended her mother's tea.

Where are Yara and Amina?

But Nylah still felt a burning sensation in her throat, so she did not voice this. Slowly, the woman moved away from them, her eyes unseeing. She disappeared into the fog of dust surrounding their place on the street.

Suddenly, Nylah's father seemed to discover a new purpose. He began moving, and his family followed close behind. Wherever wails sounded, Nylah's baba followed. As the cries grew louder, he stopped and began moving heavy metal pipes, bricks, and smoking pieces of rubble, then digging frantically with his hands. He focused all of his energy on this task, despite the dust covering his face and scratches marring his hands. After some time, he made a small noise of surprise, then quickly dug into the pile of debris and, with all of his strength, pulled.

A woman, bleeding across her face and neck, now clung to his arms.

"*Teşekkür ederim, teşekkür ederim*," she repeated with uneven breath.

Her father continued this work, following voices and instruction from other men running up and down the street to seek help for their loved ones. The word "earthquake" found Nylah's ears over and over again as she, her sister, and her mother followed their father in the cold up and down the streets of their neighborhood.

Nylah did not recognize it anymore.

Places once so lovely and familiar to her—the library, the bakery—had disappeared among the heaps of metal and stone. Tall buildings had collapsed or now leaned at unnatural angles, creaking and groaning under the strain of their own weight. No matter which way they walked, the whole city seemed distorted.

Nylah moved toward her sister and took her hand.

A PLACE OF RESPITE

After several hours, or so it seemed, they discovered a building that stood firm amid the rubble. Though she knew this was the neighborhood adjacent to their own, Nylah did not remember this place.

A woman stood in the doorway of the building's entrance, her face creased with sadness and tilted upward at the sky.

Nylah's parents slowly approached her. The woman greeted them like friends. Before they could respond, another cry sounded nearby, and Nylah's baba walked quickly away in the direction of the sound.

At this, the woman ushered the rest of the family inside. Nylah's mother nodded in response to the question on her daughters' faces. They knew not to voice their questions right now, only obey.

"Come, come," the woman said in a soft yet insistent voice.

"Sit down."

The place smelled like candle wax. Tentatively stepping further inside, Nylah glimpsed a large wooden cross overlooking the front of the room and several small candles flickering beneath it. A church, then.

"Mama, this place," Nylah began.

Her mother patted Nylah's lap, as if to say she already knew.

The woman, who had disappeared moments before, reappeared with an armful of blankets and several water bottles resting atop the pile.

Nylah's mother immediately began weeping. Unsurprised at this, the woman gently set the pile down on an empty chair near the entrance and took a seat beside her mother, pulling her into a hug.

She did not resist. Instead, Nylah's mother finally allowed her grief to emerge and leaned into the woman's embrace. Although Nylah couldn't make out all the words, she watched the woman whisper quietly into her mother's ear. Her mother nodded solemnly and held onto the woman a bit longer. Nylah glanced at her sister in question.

Does she know her?

"It feels so peaceful in this place," her mother whispered after the woman had gently released her.

"You are welcome here," she said with a wide smile, the dimple in her left cheek deepening.

The woman quietly rose again and stepped into another room. She came back after a few moments with dried fruit and nuts mixed in small, individual plastic bags.

"Why do you do this for us?" Nylah's mother asked.

"Out of love," she replied simply.

Then, after a pause: "Love for Jesus Christ and love for you."

Nylah and her family lingered in the church for a while. The woman—whose name they still did not know—invited them to stay and sleep. Before her mother could reply, Nylah's baba returned, covered in so much dust now that his hair appeared gray. He told them a relative had arrived by car to take them out of the city.

As Nylah, her mother, and Lina said goodbye, the woman asked to pray over them. Her mother did not refuse, which shocked Nylah even more than the welcome they had received.

The woman placed her hands atop the two girls' heads. Afterward, she proceeded to speak to God as no one in Nylah's memory had ever spoken to God—like a friend, like a Father. In the name of Jesus, she thanked Him for protecting their family. Then, to their collective surprise, the woman began praying over them by name. Though they had not given her their names, she mentioned each one of them, along with the names of many of the neighbors and friends they had often hosted for tea.

"We should have more supplies soon. Food, jackets, shoes, first aid," the woman told them when she finished praying.

Then, before they departed, she pulled out a book hidden under the pile of blankets she had brought in from the next room. A Christian Bible. She recommended to Nylah's mother a few sections to read. Then, she hugged her again.

As they rejoined Nylah's father and began walking in the direction of their waiting cousin, Nylah tried to recall why this woman had seemed so familiar to her. The cold night air clung to her skin and clarified her mind. She had seen her before. In their building.

She is the Christian on our floor.

So many times, Nylah recalled turning away from this woman, avoiding eye contact and lowering her head in passing. The woman always greeted her by name, and Nylah always responded with silence, as her mother told her to do.

Gazing up at her mother, her eyes wet from the chill, Nylah saw that she had recognized the woman, too. Nylah suspected that she knew as soon as they stepped into the church.

"We will read from this," her mother whispered, clutching the Bible tightly to her chest beneath the pile of blankets.

Then, as if speaking to herself, she murmured: "Her God spared her and granted her peace. I want to know about this God."

LIGHT IN THE DARKNESS

According to a report from the Center for Disaster Philanthropy, 56,000 people died in Türkiye and Syria during the 2023 earthquakes.* As cities became graveyards, the mental and physical needs of survivors multiplied. *How is God working in the midst of this challenge?* Following the earthquake, Christians in Türkiye and Syria came together to offer relief from their own limited supplies. In regions where Christians suffer a longstanding history of persecution, believers became the light, bringing hope and relief to survivors in the name of Jesus. After witnessing believers selflessly serve others, offering peace and love that defied the tragic circumstances of the earthquake, people like Nylah's mother became seekers of the one true God.

I have said these things to you, that in me you may have peace. In the world you will have tribulation. But take heart; I have overcome the world. - **John 16:33**

10

AMIR
أمير

Shortly after their rescue from ISIS, Amir and his mother, Zoya, found Amir's father, Nasir, in prison. Their captors had him arrested because of his perceived religious transgressions for marrying Zoya. Amir and his mother quickly secured Nasir's release, and over the ensuing years, the family moved countries three times in search of stability amid a region blighted by war.

At age 17, Amir had grown tall and wise beyond his years. Though the kidnapping in his youth had done unseen damage to his mind and heart, he kept moving, kept dreaming of a better life. When his father was arrested yet again, this time for poor financial dealings with untrustworthy business partners, Amir knew he had to care for his mother from then on. Amir and Zoya worked several jobs to provide for themselves. They sold all of their belongings to pay rent.

Outside of school, Amir found work assisting a kind woman in caring for her elderly father. Dalia trusted Amir completely, treating him like a younger brother. So Amir did not hesitate when she asked him to retrieve a box of packaged food that a nearby church prepared for her and her father. This surprised Amir since Dalia and her father did not attend church, and

Amir had never come across any religious items in their home. As he drove to the address Dalia gave him, Amir tried and failed to recall the last time he had stepped inside a church.

AN INVITATION

When Amir arrived, he felt overcome by the building's familiarity. The cross in the front of the room reminded him of the wooden cross that his mother had packed so gingerly into her suitcase all those years ago—before their kidnapping, before they came to this country. He recalled the prayers he had whispered in the dark of the musty room, his prison for so many months. Finally, he remembered the story his mother recounted afterward of how a picture of Jesus that she kept in her wallet had inspired the American soldiers to help her free him.

"I am here to pick up food for Dalia," Amir told the smiling man who approached him.

"Of course. Make yourself at home," the man replied.

He had a gentle face, seemingly undisturbed by the conflict that raged in the nearby streets each month. Amir realized he was the pastor.

Amir stayed at the entrance while the pastor retrieved the box. He felt drawn to the music that floated through the doors ahead of him and leaned in to hear it better.

Could worship music sound like this?

As the thought formed in his mind, Amir felt the weight of the food package on his outstretched arms.

"Would you like to stay for Bible study?" the pastor asked.

The question lingered between them as Amir considered his invitation. Though fearful of what it would mean to attend this study of the Bible, Amir desired to honor the man's kindness and show him the respect his age required. Dalia would understand his delay once he explained it to her. He sat down with the box of food in the front row of the church.

A LIFE REDEEMED

As the weeks went by, Amir found himself coming to the church over and over again. He couldn't identify why, but for some reason, he felt drawn back each week. He listened to the pastor's message, then lost himself in the worship music. He found it incredibly comforting.

As the worship drew to a close one evening, Amir remained in the pew in contemplation. Something shifted inside him as he reflected on everything the pastor had said. He didn't want to leave.

After some time in the pew, the pastor approached him again, taking a seat beside him in the pew.

"Do you know Jesus?" he asked Amir bluntly.

"Of course."

But that is a lie.

From his long silence, Amir suspected the pastor knew.

Still, in his most confident-sounding voice, Amir shared with the pastor all that he could recall about Jesus from stories his mother once told him. But he left untold the story of his kidnapping and rescue.

The pastor listened to Amir patiently, nodding his head at times in agreement with Amir's assertions. But something must have passed beyond the façade between them to prompt the pastor to say his next words.

"Maybe the time has come for you to start living your life with Jesus," he said softly.

Amir didn't know why, but tears began to slip down his cheeks.

At that moment, the pastor fell to his knees. He took Amir's hands in his and gazed up at his face. It startled Amir that the pastor would kneel before another man, a stranger no less, and he tried to tell him not to bother—that he didn't need Jesus. But Amir's voice faltered, and he realized that he did not believe the lie anymore.

"Let us stop talking and pray," the pastor urged.

Amir moved to his knees, too, and, together, they prayed. When they finished, Amir felt something stirring inside of him: he wanted to give his whole being to Jesus.

TEN YEARS LATER

"After that prayer in the chapel, the pastors who welcomed me to my first Bible study baptized me into the family of God. With great patience, they discipled and mentored me in the faith. They helped me to understand the

Word of God and how to live a life with Jesus—a life *for* Jesus.

I wanted everyone to know the wonder of this life with Jesus, so I talked about Him everywhere I went. I shared my faith without reservation, so much so that the Muslim authorities became aware of my choice to follow Jesus. When they contacted me to tell me that my public declaration of faith amounted to an abdication of my lineage to Mohammed, the memories of being locked in that room for months as a child rushed back. That was why our kidnappers hated us so much.

So, choosing to be a part of the family of Christ meant choosing to let go of any rights I had to the family of Mohammed. So they had me sign papers, stating my choice and its implications. Signing my name to that paper was like signing for my freedom.

At the church, my new brothers and sisters in Christ embraced me. They encouraged me. They recognized gifts in me and invited me to use them to help others understand the Bible, especially children. Though I eventually moved countries again, I found a new church, and I served as a children's Bible teacher there, putting into practice what I had learned.

I couldn't see it at the time, but I see it now—God's mercy and presence throughout my life. He was there even in the most difficult of times. It was God I spoke to in my captivity, even though I did not know Him then. And He was listening. Even when I didn't believe, He rescued me; the face of His Son moved the soldiers to action. After that, He led me to a job that would take me into a church on the night of their Bible study. It was God who drew me back to that church again and again. It was God who moved that pastor I did not know to fall on his knees and pray with me for my salvation. And it was God who answered, God who saved me.

By His grace, not only did I finish my high school exams, but I earned an undergraduate degree, enabling me to do the work I do now, and best of all, to work for another brother in Christ."

Eli nodded, his eyes wide and dreamlike from listening to Amir's testimony. The two young men sat in front of the untouched pita wraps they had bought from a street vendor and taken back to the office on their lunch break. Eli had asked Amir when they returned to their desks how he came to know Christ. An hour later, the food remained untouched.

"What did you take away from your years of teaching?" Eli asked.

Amir thought for some time before replying.

"I was happy when my students made it to Grade 5, but after that, they had nowhere to go," Amir said. "And I realized that the teenage refugees all around us need a school, too."

His stomach growled audibly, so Eli finally moved toward his pita filled with lamb and tzatziki. Pausing just before the first bite, he glanced up at Amir, eyes bright.

"Write a proposal for the school."

Amir gaped at Eli, who had moved on to his lunch, happily munching. When Eli said no more, Amir's mind filled with exciting images of a Christian school for teenage refugees.

Several months passed, months bursting with the busyness of holidays and family gatherings that kept Amir always on the brink of writing the proposal but never with the clarity of mind to go through with it.

One morning, a verse came to him that gave him the boldness to try.

With God all things are possible.

Arriving at the office earlier than normal, Amir settled into his desk, opened his laptop, and started typing. His vision for the school—brightly colored classrooms, soothing, blue uniforms, caring, devoted teachers who loved the students with the love of Jesus and spoke of Him every day— seemed to flow from his fingers and onto the keyboard. The proposal came together so quickly that Amir felt certain of God's help in the task.

Lord, I commit this to you and ask for your sovereign guidance.

After praying over the single-paged document for several minutes, Amir clicked open his email, typed a brief introduction, then sent it to an organization he knew served refugee camps outside the city.

Twenty days later, Amir received a short message from the leaders of the organization.

The school is approved.

LIGHT IN THE DARKNESS

According to a 2022 UN report, 30% of school-aged Syrian refugee children (ages 6-17) in Lebanon have never been to school. Schools like the one Amir envisioned remain rare, and currently, 100 students are enrolled at this school with hundreds more on a waiting list, all teenage refugees from a Muslim background.[10] *How is God working in the midst of this challenge?* The school's teachers actively pursue discipleship relationships with their students, recognizing what they face—the dangers of war, ISIS, economic pressures, and family conflict, which Amir experienced firsthand. But these struggles grew in Amir the passion with which he now oversees the school and seeks to see all of its students discipled. He knows from experience that, no matter their circumstance, God can raise up children as spiritual leaders so that the gospel goes forth to all the nations.

Kings of the earth and all peoples, princes and all rulers of the earth! Young men and maidens together, old men and children! Let them praise the name of the Lord, for his name alone is exalted; his majesty is above earth and heaven. - **Psalm 148:11-13**

A LETTER FROM JOHN

Having grown up in the MENA region, I have a deep, personal understanding of the unique challenges MENA children face on a daily basis. In my childhood, I attended a school of about 3,000 students, the majority of whom were Muslim, with some nominal Christians. As one of the only Christians in the school, I became a target for the other children to ridicule and treat me harshly. I did not fit in because of my faith, and for two years, I lived in fear of being beaten up because of what I believed. That constant fear and isolation grew harder and harder to endure, but by God's grace, my faith did not waver.

During that time, I befriended a classmate from a different religious background and invited him to attend church with me. Through this relationship, he came to know Jesus as his Lord and Savior. God then went on to use this same boy to bring 14 other students to the Lord, all while he endured extreme persecution and, following a brutal beating, prolonged isolation from his own family.

Stories like these are common throughout the MENA region. It is my hope that anyone who reads this book considers the reality of the hardships children in the MENA region experience and how God enables them to persevere amid terrible difficulties to draw others to Himself. I have consistently seen lives transformed by glimpses of God's light in the darkness. In the lives of the children...in the lives of those around them...in the lives of those now reading their stories.

Thank you to the children and their families for lending us these stories and to the Ananias House staff for your hard work and dedication in writing them down for this book. You have served the Lord well.

John Samara
Founder, Executive Director
Ananias House

BE A LIGHT

Do you want to fellowship with Christians who follow Jesus through war, persecution, and oppression? Ananias House bridges the distance between believers in the West and the growing body of Christ in the Middle East and North Africa (MENA) through prayer, Bible training, and physical and spiritual resources to build up God's global family in an increasingly hostile world. The stories included in this book only scratch the surface of what God is doing in the lives of MENA children—and the men and women they grow up to be.

You are invited to come alongside these believers today by:
1. Heading to **www.ananiashouse.org** to download our free resources. You'll learn about honor-shame culture, the impact of Islam on the MENA region, and the biblical significance of that region.
2. Joining our ministry through monthly gifts. You will help build up growing MENA churches and gain access to powerful stories of God working through MENA Christians on the mission field.
3. Becoming emboldened to live out your faith in Jesus every day with the spiritual encouragement of believers persevering across the world.

Finally, we encourage you to write to us at **contact@ananiashouse.org**, as well as to join us in praying that every child in the Middle East and North Africa would encounter God. Together, let's pray that through their eyes, the hope of Jesus shines onto the world around them.

LET US PRAY

Our Father, who art in heaven,
Hallowed be thy Name.
Thy Kingdom come.
Thy will be done
On earth, as it is in heaven.
Give us this day our daily bread.
And forgive us our trespasses,
As we forgive those who trespass against us.
And lead us not into temptation,
But deliver us from evil.
For thine is the kingdom,
And the power, and the glory,
Forever and ever.
Amen.

NOTES

1. "New Kidnapping Trends on the Global Stage." *HOSTAGE US*, https://hostageus.org/new-kidnapping-trends-on-the-global-stage. Accessed 25 May 2023.
2. United Nations Children's Fund, *Child Marriage in the Middle East and North Africa* - Updated February 2022, UNICEF Regional Office for the Middle East and North Africa, Amman, February 2022. https://www.unicef.org/mena/media/17696/file/ChildMarriage-Factsheet-Feb22.pdf%20.pdf.
3. Alzaghoul, Aseel F., et al. "Post-Traumatic Stress Disorder Interventions for Children and Adolescents Affected by War in Low- and Middle-Income Countries in the Middle East: Systematic Review." *BJPsych Open*, vol. 8, no. 5, 2022, p. e153., doi:10.1192/bjo.2022.552.
4. Hauch, Lars. "Sharia law will play a greater role in Syria's future." *Middle East Eye*, 16 June 2016, https://www.middleeasteye.net/opinion/sharia-law-will-play-greater-role-syrias-future. Accessed 25 May 2022.
5. United Nations, General Assembly Security Council, *Children and armed conflict: report of the Secretary General*, A/76/871-S/2022/493 (23 June 2022). https://documents-dds-ny.un.org/doc/UNDOC/GEN/N22/344/71/PDF/N2234471.pdf?OpenElement.
6. Institute for Economics & Peace. Global Peace Index 2022: Measuring Peace in a Complex World, Sydney, June 2022. Available from: http://visionofhumanity.org/resources (25 May 2023).
7. United Nations High Commission for Refugees, World Food Programme, UNICEF (2022). *Lebanon: Vulnerability Assessment of Syrian Refugees in Lebanon*, 2022. Accessed from: https://microdata.unhcr.org.
8. United Nations Children's Fund, *Violent Beginnings: Children growing up in Lebanon's crisis*, UNICEF, Lebanon, December 2021 https://www.unicef.org/lebanon/media/7626/file.
9. "2023 Turkey-Syria Earthquake." *Center for Disaster Philanthropy*, Updated 23 May 2023, https://disasterphilanthropy.org/disasters/2023-turkey-syria-earthquake. Accessed 23 May 2023.
10. United Nations High Commission for Refugees, World Food Programme, UNICEF (2022). *Lebanon: Vulnerability Assessment of Syrian Refugees in Lebanon*, 2022. Accessed from: https://microdata.unhcr.org.

The song lyrics included in Chapter 2 are from the 1878 hymn "It is Well With My Soul" by Horatio Gates Spafford.